Paradise and Pestilence

Paradise and Pestilence

ASPECTS OF PROVENCE

Suzanne, Duchess of St Albans

PETER OWEN
London & Chester Springs PA

© PETER OWEN PUBLISHERS
73 Kenway Road London SW5 ORE

Peter Owen books are distributed in the USA by
Dufour Editions Inc. Chester Springs PA 19425–0007

First published in Great Britain 1997
© Suzanne St Albans 1997

A catalogue record for this book is available
from the British Library

ISBN 0–7206–1027–3

Printed in Great Britain by
Biddles of Guildford and King's Lynn

Contents

Menu
—
Hors d' œuvre
Dinde truffée
Asperges glacées
Pâté de foie gras
Plum pudding
Macédoine de fruits.
au Champagne
Liqueurs
—

Noël 1921

for Charles

whose idea it was that I should write this book

CHAPTER 1

Goodbye to All That

As the north wind came howling across the terrace under a pewter-coloured sky, a few limp stalks fluttered from the pots and tubs of long-dead summer flowers. Whipped about by the gale, strands of Russian vine lashed around like angry snakes, and snowdrifts raced across the huge four-leaf clover I had painted on the terrace floor in its heyday. Through the dusty double glazing of the drawing-room windows, I stared at the writhing plane trees on the Embankment. Beyond them the heaving yellow waters of the river Thames rushed headlong between their frozen banks.

Adding to all this desolation, our ultra-modern central-heating plant had broken down, and the thermostat registered below freezing point. An unusually frostbound winter is not the best time to move house.

The hour had come. I had to go. Parked in Cheyne Walk, my Mini was buried in snow. But, staunch as ever, it started up at once. Day after day, between spells of feverish packing, I was driving over to Moorfields Hospital to see Charles, who was recovering from a double cataract operation. With both his eyes wrapped up in plastic, he was flat on his back, lying there in a state of hopeless boredom. Nobody knew if he would ever see again. With his macabre sense of humour, the surgeon would only say 'Wait and see'.

I arrived to find a nurse changing Charles's dressings. 'If you go to the waiting room, I'll call you when I've finished,' she said.

My spirits dropped to zero as I sat hunched in the mid-morning twilight of the dismal room. Eventually the nurse bustled in with all her starch creaking and crackling around

her. 'He's ready – you can go in now. And take this, it will
cheer you up.'

'What is it?' I asked as she dropped something cold, round
and smooth into my hand.

'A glass eyeball. We put them into the eye sockets of the
dead before the relatives come to take leave of their dear
departed. It will bring you luck.'

Staring at the gruesome, incredibly lifelike object, all blood-
shot with a network of little red veins, I thanked her. The
sight of it on that cold, dark January morning sent my morale
up several notches. Feeling much better I dropped it into my
purse.

When Charles left hospital, his ordeal was far from over.
Allergic to the drops they had given him, his eyes turned
purple, swelled and bulged, and looked more like stewed
plums as the days went by. Quite unable to open them,
he had to be led everywhere by the hand. And it was in
this condition that he supervised the final throes of the
move.

Staged in arctic temperatures, the packing took place on
the dark green carpet of the dining-room floor. Scabby black
tin trunks left over from the last century gaped wide open,
steaming with camphor fumes. All round, the family silver
lay in heaps. Rare tomes bound in sheepskin stood un-
steadily in tottering piles next to the miniatures in their
blue velvet mounts. These were going to the bank for safe-
keeping and for the benefit of future heirs.

The cold was penetrating. As I crawled on hands and knees
among the trunks, Charles stamped about to keep his feet
warm, issuing orders.

'This is to go to Child's Bank. That you will take to France,
and this lot can go to Murray.' From time to time he trod on
the service bell under the carpet. 'Blast, there's someone at
the door. You'd better go and see.' Or else, 'Who the hell
can it be? I can't possibly see anyone now.'

Our ex-butler, Hung-Ta, the good angel of the house for so
many years, had persuaded his new boss to give him a day
off to help us with the packing. He staggered down the stairs
with another black trunk in his arms.

Moth balls shot off in all directions as Charles's resplendent
Grand Falconer's court dress was shaken out. Embossed from

top to toe with acorns and oakleaves of solid gold, it was so heavy I could hardly lift it. Then came the jaunty black hat and an empty scabbard. When I mentioned this, Charles announced that nobody ever went to court with a sword. The bulky coronation robes were shaken out and folded back into their ancient tissue paper, as soft and fine as silk handkerchiefs.

As I had never worn my own robes, I tried them on that evening in the cold, dark, empty house. The long red velvet dress with Chantilly lace down the front was a perfect fit. The huge train hooked on to the shoulders, spreading several yards behind. Over this went a short white fur cape decorated with four rows of small black ermine tails. Last of all came the coronets, the largest of which was a proper self-respecting crown. It sank right down over my head like a tea-cosy. My own pigmy version sat on top of my head, with huge iron pins hanging all round like a crown of thorns.

Thus rigged out, I trailed through the echoing house, down the stairs and in and out of every room. Here the ancestral portraits used to hang on the golden wallpaper. On the top floor, drawings and engravings had lined the landing like postage stamps. Further down the staircase, Lady Diana Beauclerk's delicate watercolours from the Strawberry Hill collection had clustered edge to edge. The Wedgwood-blue drawing room had housed the eighteenth-century pastel portraits, the hall and the dining room the life-size oils of noble forebears back to the fourteenth century.

Into the icy ballroom I finally tottered, banging my shins against the last surviving chairs. A sudden ring at the front door made me jump. Hanging on to my wobbling coronet and feeling rather an ass, I crept through the gloom and opened the door a crack.

'Gorblimey,' gasped the man on the doorstep, looking as if he had seen a ghost.

And before I could utter, he streaked off as fast as he could down the slippery, snow-covered pavement.

Charles had flown to Nice, and the day had come to load the Mini with our last remaining chattels for the trip to the South. Good as her word, Mary Pless turned up to help pack the car. Hung-Ta, who had taken yet another day off, was there as well, a pearl beyond price.

Having dumped everything outside on the pavement, we gloomily eyed the enormous pile. There were books, records, pictures, pots and pans, clothes and a huge case of silver. Charles's hi-fi equipment, which ran to four bulky units, came in the most impossible shapes and sizes.

'How on earth will it all fit in?' I groaned in despair.

'Don't worry too much,' said Hung-Ta. 'Quite easy, quite easy.'

'Is he good at this sort of thing?' Mary asked.

'Absolutely brilliant. Just wait and see.'

'Chinese puzzles and all that sort of thing, I suppose,' she said, picking up an armful of books.

Within half an hour Hung-Ta had the entire lot stowed away, the hi-fi speakers in the back, the turntable strapped into the passenger seat beside me and the radio on the floor leaning against the gear lever. Wedged in with a bundle of paperbacks, the silver was lodged in the boot. The rest, crammed in here and there, gradually rose to the roof.

'You must be able to see out of your back window,' said Mary, looking worried.

Hung-Ta poked a hole through with his fist and said, 'Quite all right now, quite all right. You can see quite enough, quite enough.'

I squeezed into the driver's seat with an electric kettle poking into the back of my neck. It was all so closely packed that I could hardly twitch an eyebrow without causing a landslide, and in this state I set off along the Embankment.

'Take no notice of the roads, just follow the signs,' Hansel Pless had said the previous evening. His advice worked admirably: I was in Dover a couple of hours later, just in time to sweep into the bowels of the *Merry Mermaid* for a bumpy Channel crossing.

After three long days of slithering along the ice-plated roads of central France, I finally reached Vence, where the sun was shining bright and hot. But a fast-running torrent, the result of recent downpours, gushed along the steep track leading up to Mas Mistral. Undaunted, the Mini, used by now to such conditions, attacked the flowing stream.

Sitting in the sun round the garden table by the cypress trees were my sister and her French husband Pierre and Charles, who had arrived a few days earlier. He was in tremendous form and already suntanned. With his eyesight completely restored, he would not even have to wear glasses any more. Patrick Trevor-Roper had performed one more of his many miracles.

Immensely relieved at having reached the end of my odyssey, I joined them for lunch. The local white wine flowed comfortingly under the hot winter sun. Totally uninterested in my adventures, they were engrossed in their own schemes for restoring the house to its former glory.

'What we must do,' Charles was saying, 'is make all those separate parts into properly self-contained flats and then let them off for the summer.'

'Good idea,' said Anne. 'And now that we are all here, we can get down to work at once.'

'Everything needs painting. Look at all those scabby shutters.'

'We mustn't forget the garden,' said Pierre. 'There's a lot of clearing to be done.'

Yes, I thought, at least two acres of back-breaking work in sight. My mind reeled at the thought. After two glasses of wine, I already felt light-headed. Stretching out my legs, I leaned my aching back against the iron chair. An early frog, trying out his voice, croaked a couple of times in the undergrowth. A green bird perched on the telephone wire was composing an elaborate tune which went on and on and on. The last thing I felt like was jungle-clearing and painting shutters. But obviously, since we had all come home to roost in the old family house built by my parents in the early twenties, the job would have to be done. Since their death several years before, the property had been abandoned to its own devices and badly needed a face-lift. But at least it was still standing and ready to give us a roof over our heads, leaky though it might be in parts. I swallowed another glass of wine and closed my eyes.

When I opened them again the sun had set and everybody had vanished. With a jolt I realised I was back in mountain climate – blistering in the sun and freezing out of it.

The next day we got down to work in earnest. Some years before, the house, too big for my parents in post-war conditions, had been split up into various parts. The west wing, being the smallest and least forbidding, was to come first on the resurrection list. The temperature was near to zero and it was only with frequent swigs of white wine that we managed to keep going at all. But within a week the job was done: bedrooms, bathroom, kitchen, dining room, drawing room, vestibule, all gleaming white and reeking with the poisonous fumes of paint.

Next came the south-facing flat with its high ceilings and french windows. But before we could tackle that, drastic surgery was needed. The huge twisted coils of wistaria as thick as a wrestler's thighs, which climbed up the front of the house, had to be severely amputated. They had crept under the roof, displacing tiles and causing floods and dry rot. Hacking at them was like trying to bisect writhing serpents that knocked you almost unconscious in the process. Then there was the moonflower creeper firmly welded to the shutters with its millions of little suction pads.

Eventually, on a blazing February day, it was all finished and ready for letting as soon as possible in order to justify the expense and to keep the exchequer afloat.

The time had now come to start clearing the grounds. Every day the sun rose a little earlier. Wild violets were springing up like a purple lawn all round the house. As we sat in the sun as usual, lapping white wine at the lunch table, the garden, washed clean by the previous night's downpour, gleamed with a hundred varieties of green.

'I can't wait to get my mower back,' said Charles, whose machine, mangled over the years by my father's hopeless gardeners, regularly broke down every few days.

Pierre's favourite gadget was a petrol-powered scythe, a cunning Japanese device with many fiendish tricks of its own. Strapped over one shoulder, this infernally smelly contraption had already scorched away most of the skin on Pierre's right arm.

Back from the kitchen, Anne came tripping across the uneven ground, towing the lunch trolley rattling with glass and bouncing crockery.

'And when the garden is tidied up and the whole house crawling with tenants,' she said, laying the table, 'we'll all go off to Italy for a holiday.'

'Let's find the tenants first,' I said.

'Oh, there'll be no problem about that. The moment people hear about all those beautiful flats, they'll come in droves.'

Right on cue, and if anybody can believe such a coincidence, a couple of figures appeared, strolling up the drive.

Although we had last seen him in London many years before, it was impossible not to recognize Desmond at once. The only difference was that his new wife, Helen, was with him. It turned out they had a house in St Jeannet, at the foot of the great sombre rock of the Baou. They were on holiday, between two sets of tenants.

'You let your house?' I screeched. 'How do you set about it?'

'Come to lunch on Sunday and we'll introduce you to the man who finds the tenants.'

Another bottle appeared, followed by several more. Like the loaves and the fishes, the food multiplied of its own accord as all our greedy jaws dealt with Anne's delicious cuisine. Desmond, who is an 'old soul', embarked on his favourite topic, his latest visit to the retreat, where mystics assemble to meditate and send out world-saving vibrations into the cosmos.

Charles and Desmond's wife were rattling off more and more nonsense as the wine went down, and Helen's beautiful brown bosom heaved and quivered with mirth at his outrageous witticisms.

Sunday dawned bright and clear and as hot as any fine day in February can be. We drove through woods full of bustling birds and wild cyclamen, past the trout farm and the old mill, until at last there was the villa nestling in its tangled garden. Lunch was laid out on the terrace, and David, the man who found the tenants, was there to meet us.

We tucked into an ample Irish meal *à la provençale*, all delightfully full of *imprévu*. A dozen cats, surrounded by a mewing mob of kittens, crawled around our legs, hissing like snakes and snatching at every crumb that came their way. Fascinated, I watched a minute kitten gobble up an olive, stone and all.

'Whatever do you do with them when you go back to Ireland?' I asked.

'David stuffs them into a sack,' said Helen, 'then he dumps them near a block of flats somewhere along the coast. So they get fed and looked after by all the tenants.'

I looked at David, and he winked at me. Knowing my Southerners as I do, I thought it more likely the cats would get a good kick whenever they appeared. But there would be dustbins from which they could scratch a living.

Desmond, an expert on esoteric lore, author of *Flying Saucers Have Landed* and many other books on the subject, showed us photos of elementals, tree sprites and Little People of one kind and another. Launched on his favourite topic, he pointed a long bony finger at the Baou. 'This rock is particularly magnetic,' he said. 'I have seldom felt the emanations of a magic mountain run up my nerves like this. Stretch out your hands. Can you feel anything?' he asked.

'Not a thing,' I said firmly. Later, however, Desmond was to introduce me to a stone whose vibrations were so powerful that I eventually ended up in hospital.

Finally getting round to our burning problem, we tackled David about it. Before we left, he agreed to come and 'view our accommodation'.

In due course he turned up at Mas Mistral. Anne and I were on our knees, wrenching out weeds and sticking geranium cuttings into the mud.

'I'm afraid there aren't many flowers out yet,' said my sister apologetically.

'*You* are the flowers, my dear,' he said.

'What a nice man,' purred Anne, scrambling to her feet. 'Come and have a look at the house. All newly painted and lovely and fresh,' she crooned, wiping her muddy hands on her jeans.

We led him into the ice-cold west-wing flat. Compared to what it was before we started, it looked absolutely splendid. At least it did to us.

'Hum,' said David. 'Not very cosy. Good God! Look at that crack in the kitchen wall!'

The crack was left over from the last earthquake, and I had tried to stuff it with putty, but this had shrunk with drying and, once more, daylight shone through like a mocking grin.

'Don't worry about that,' Anne said airily. 'All it needs is a bit of plaster. My husband is just about to do it.'

'I'll have to come back and take photographs and measurements,' said David. 'But I doubt very much that I can help you. My tenants are *very* particular.'

'Well, let's go over and see the other flat,' said Anne in sprightly tones. The sun, fortunately, was streaming in through the french windows.

'My Gawd!' exclaimed David again, staring at the floor in the hall. 'You do go in for cracks, don't you?'

'Oh, that's just wistaria roots pushing up through the foundations,' I told him casually. 'Take no notice.'

He looked at the bedrooms in silence. 'A bit unusual, if I may say so,' he muttered, staring at the ceilings, scarlet in one room, purple in another and bright green in the hall. At least they kept his attention away from the woodworm in the parquet floor. But in the kitchen he gasped, 'Oh dear, this is very sad! A downright disaster! This will never do.' My heart sank out of sight.

'You'll have to lower the ceiling, cover up those pipes, do something about this, that and the other . . .'

I stopped listening.

'The central heating works very well,' said Anne quickly.

'We're hardly planning on using that at Easter, I trust,' David snapped. Anne's face drooped.

'And this, I suppose, is the dining room? A bit poky, wouldn't you say?'

'We've had twelve to fifteen people eating here many times,' I snarled, my blood rising.

We progressed to the bathroom.

'And this is . . . Oh dear, oh dear, oh dear!'

'At least the shower doesn't spray you whenever you pull the plug, as always happens in Turkey,' I said.

'This is the glamorous Riviera, hardly the wilds of Turkey,' David remarked severely.

'Let's go and have a drink,' Anne suggested quickly.

After David had left, she stared at me with her great oyster-coloured eyes. 'It's no good is it? He won't do a thing for us!'

'It's a technique. Don't worry. They all do it. Let's wait and see.'

CHAPTER 2

Les Baux

THE glorious weather of early February disappeared behind heavy thunderclouds, and our famous winter *précipitations* were upon us. During these periods of tropical rainfall, it can go on pounding out of the sky for days on end. Before work could be resumed, our garden, which ran with swirling rivers of mud, would have to dry off. To make the most of these soggy days, Anne and I decided to go and visit the medieval fortress of Les Baux. Whereupon the rain turned to snow, and overnight the mountainside was transformed into an alpine landscape glittering under a brilliant, cloudless sky.

Early one very cold morning found us stamping about in the snow outside the Régence café in Vence's main square at 4.45 a.m. Cocooned in sheepskin and shod in fur-lined snowboots, we waited for our coach to the west. Only half an hour late, it came gliding into the square like a fish, gleaming with hoarfrost, silver white in the glaring light of the moon. Thankfully we climbed into its muggy warmth, and off we set on our long drive to the legendary feudal stronghold.

For four hours we sped through a moonscape where snow-bound fields, trees and sky all merged into the same dead white, eerie light. As this slowly changed to a dim, cheerless winter dawn, a crag of pale rock suddenly appeared like some huge ghost wrapped in its shroud of snow, floating in the dead landscape. Great gaunt boulders, carved into weird, tormented shapes followed. The vertical cliffs, all split and twisted into pillars and chasms, rose to the roots of the fortress above. No vegetation grows in this arid desolation haunted only by bats and witches. And hidden away somewhere in this nightmare stage set lies the Treasure of the Golden

Goat, buried by the gods and never found to this day.

The gorge of Les Baux was beginning to close in on us. Anchored on top of the rugged outcrop of the Alpilles, the old ruin stuck up into the sky like the splintered remains of some prehistoric petrified forest. Lying about in grandiose disorder were huge white blocks of limestone that had crashed from their towers over the ages. Judging by the massive, scattered foundations, the castle of Les Baux must have been as extensive as the Palace of the Popes at Avignon.

Winding spiral stairs, exposed to the open sky, climbed blindly into the racing clouds of dawn. Sweeping about over the ancient ruin, crows, upright on their tails, yarked angrily at the wind. Enormous dungeons, their sides cracked open, reached down to the heart of the mountain. No one had yet explored the furthest depths of those caverns to collect the crumbling bones of long-dead prisoners.

Unable to go further, the coach stopped at the foot of the great rock. From there it is a steep climb into the middle of the town. By now blowing furiously, the wind howled round every corner as it whipped through the narrow streets, round houses all built of the same dour rock out of which they sprang.

Rue Trencat had been dug out of the mountain by the Romans, who left a trail of coins behind to prove that they had passed this way. As the view from here extends as far as Camargue and the huge expanse of the Rhône Delta, any raiding party landing along the coast would have been spotted at once by the castle watch. The position was impregnable.

The icy wind, shrieking through the streets, drove us into the church. Built in the tenth century, it was as bare and cheerless as the grave. And it was here, by the altar of the Madonna, that a mane of golden hair (now in the Arles museum) was found intact beneath one of the tombstones. When the grave was opened, a young girl, dressed in bridal apparel, was found buried there, lying in angelic serenity with a book of hours in her hands. All but the golden tresses had fallen to dust on contact with the air.

Princess Strella of Florence, who had come as a bride to the seneschal of the fortress, had died (of fright, no doubt) at the very sight of the grim surroundings in which she was to spend the rest of her days. The shock, after her native Florence, so full of festivals, music and dancing, was too fearful

to bear, and the poor creature had expired before her wedding day.

The denuded tenth-century church exuded a feeling of haughty
grandeur. It was easy to imagine the lords of the citadel,
encased in full armour, stamping into High Mass, grunting
and cursing as they shambled up to the altar for communion
under the glaring eye of their confessor.

The cold was penetrating. Craving warmth, we dived into
the only café we could find in the deserted little town.

'Do you get a lot of people here at this time of year?' I
asked the owner.

'No tourists, a few schools turn up. And they used to bring
parties of *troisième âge*' – senior citizens, to us – 'until one of
them collapsed and died last year,' he said.

'Killed by the cold?' I asked sympathetically.

'So they said. It was quite an *histoire*, as the rest of the
party refused to take the corpse back on the bus with them.
I can't say I blamed them.'

'What happened then?'

'We had to keep him here until the undertaker came to
collect him next day.'

'How long has the place been a shambles like this?'

'Ever since Cardinal Richelieu knocked it down.'

'Was anyone living in the castle at the time?'

'Yes, the Comte de Villeneuve was in residence.'

'You mean the Seigneur of Vence?'

'That's the man. He wouldn't let anyone through the gate,
even when they tried to send in the troops dressed as nuns.'

'So they knocked it down?'

'Bit by bit. But it took them a whole year. After that the
French King gave the ruin to Prince Honoré de Grimaldi, and
the Princes of Monaco have been Marquis des Baux ever
since.

The Lords of Les Baux, for some reason known only to
themselves, claimed descent from King Balthazar, one of the
three wise men of the East. And from them they took their
crazy motto *'Au hazard Balthazar'*. I asked what that was
supposed to mean.

'Nothing at all. It was just a war-cry. On their coat of arms
they had the star with sixteen rays that led the shepherds to
the stable. The gypsies, by the way, use the same symbol.
Out of all this, make what you will,' concluded my man.

These fierce robber barons, as uncompromising as their fortress, were an exotic bunch of ruffians. Princes of Cephalonia, Neophantis, Taranto and Achaia, Counts of Spoleto, Avelin and Montecoglioso, they were also Podestats of Arles and Milan and Emperors of Constantinople. Or so they claimed. In spite of all these grandiose titles, they were as savage as their surrounding rocks, over which you can see wild boar galloping to this day. Throughout its history the turbulent brood was involved in constant battles, raids and slaughter, leaving chaos and desolation in their wake wherever they went. They scooped up beautiful princesses here and there but only married those who were great heiresses as well. These mountain pirates were the most uncouth and barbaric medieval barons ever to wield a lance.

In this formidable fortress, which had bred so many war-lords, the women tried the best they could to find some form of entertainment to relieve the grim condition of their lives. The high-vaulted rooms were ice-cold as soon as you got away from the roaring tree trunks blazing away in the great fireplaces. Raging draughts howled through halls and passages, all hung with trophies, hauberks and chain mail, arbalests and heavy Turkish swords from the Crusades. You could never get away from the brutish atmosphere of the fortress.

When they could find no husband worthy of their noble blood, the women went into convents. But on the whole, if a suitable warlord could be found for them, they much preferred the rough and tumultuous life to which they were bred.

Troubadours, coming into their own around this time, were their salvation. Stephanette, as the reigning Countess of Les Baux and daughter of Count Gilbert of Provence, was a lady of substance and prestige. Her husband owned no fewer than seventy-nine towns, castles and fortresses in the surrounding territory.

At Les Baux she set up a court of love, which she proceeded to conduct with fastidious elegance and Byzantine finesse. The most prominent troubadours soon came flocking to her colours, and before long other castles were setting up their own courts of love as well. The fashion was spreading fast, and Stephanette was soon established as the founder of the new vogue. But in spite of all her careful vigilance, matters began to go wrong. The troubadour Gilhelm de Cabestan elected as his leading lady one Tricline de Carbonelle, whose husband, quite by chance, happened to be in love with her. Wild with jealousy, he slew poor Gilhelm and had his heart dished up for dinner. When he told Tricline that she had just eaten her lover's heart, she said it tasted so good that she never wanted to eat anything else again. Rushing to the window, she threw herself out of the tower, crashing on the rocks several hundred feet below. To this day wine from this area is called Troubadour's Blood. Fortunately for all concerned, most husbands much preferred guerrilla warfare, raping, plundering and other such delights, to domestic bliss. So they were only too happy to offload their wives into the arms of troubadours.

Another member of the club who distinguished himself had his tongue slit for talking too much. When it was healed and he recovered the gift of the gab, he set his cap at a lady known as the She-Wolf of Provence. Hoping to win her heart, he dressed up in the freshly stripped skin of a male wolf. And so, dripping with blood and stinking to high heaven, he scrambled across the mountains to conquer his love. But, alas, shepherds were there with their dogs as well. Scenting the hated enemy, the sheepdogs set upon Vidal and savaged him almost to death. So it was a very mangled suitor who landed on his lady's doorstep that night.

And so it went on, loose morals being happily encouraged by the class system of the Middle Ages. Marriage, based on sound business arrangements, usually lasted for life. It brought together lands, castles and great feudal fortunes for the benefit of both parties. The nobility did as they pleased, and the troubadours glorified their freedom from religious morality. With a few exceptions, medieval barons, who arranged their affairs to suit themselves, sensibly accepted their wives' plans, and there were no more suicides or murders than at any other time in history.

Fin Amor was mental adultery (in theory, anyway), which became more refined and purified as it grew more passionate. Troubadours thought of themselves as high priests and missionaries. Their ladies stood for eternal light, an image of chastity liberating the soul from the prison of the flesh. All very pure, high-minded and virtuous, in intention at least. But the daughters of the haughty barons of Les Baux often needed stronger meat than this flimsy diet of sighs and hopes and never-never love. Left on their own for months, sometimes years on end, they had nothing to do. Cooking and house-work (such as it was) fell to slaves and other menials. Infants were looked after by wet nurses, then sent off to 'boarding school' in other castles, where, as pageboys and ladies-in-waiting, they were taught their medieval manners. These lonely women could hardly be blamed for trying to liven up the gloomy bleakness of castle life.

Troubadours, who first appeared as itinerant songwriters and entertainers in Languedoc, with a hurdy-gurdy on their back, helped to maintain the courts of love in medieval castles for over two hundred years. Like calypso writers, they made up their songs on the spur of the moment, using local events of the day as their subject matter. Told in verse and set to music, these ditties were as addictive then as our daily news on television is to us today. In a certain mood, troubadours also claimed that Provençal poetry was connected with alchemy and the occult. They insisted that only a few people understood the hidden, esoteric message of their lyrics. These, they claimed, had a double meaning, a kind of code addressed to the initiated. *Gai savoir* was about the sacred arts. *Noble savoir* concerned heraldry and other such mundane matters. Well, anything is possible, including the thought that these romantic trou-badours may have been a bit of a fraud as well.

One way or another, they had come to the end of their run. The age of the courts of love was over, and the era of all these delightful, if inane, pastimes finally came to an end through the crusade led by the Pope and the King of France against the Cathar heresy in the early thirteenth century.

In place of troubadours came fierce inquisitors, travelling monks checking up on the morals and religious views of the barons and their ladies and a new breed of incorruptible clerics who kept a stern eye on the affairs of their parish. If the troubadours achieved nothing else, they did at least contribute to the reform of the clergy in the south. It was the unruly behaviour of the local priesthood that had driven the populations of Languedoc and Provence to switch their allegiance from the Church to the Cathars, whose morals were a shining example of selflessness and total dedication to the service of humanity as long as they lived. But some of their beliefs differed from those of the Church, so, as heretics, they had to be exterminated.

CHAPTER 3

Early Times

THE day after we returned from Les Baux, everybody was invited to a *vin d'honneur* (drinks on the house) at the Château de Villeneuve in Vence. Maître Hugues, the leading lawyer of the area and owner of the château, had left it to the town in his will when he died a few months earlier.

A municipal library had been established on the ground floor, and a room upstairs, handed over to the British community for the same purpose, was already filled with a handsome collection of books in English. This was indeed something to celebrate. From then on, spending most of my spare time in one or the other of these two libraries, I began to read through the history of Provence in earnest.

When you start to delve into its past, what strikes you most about it is the bewildering succession of disasters, catastrophes, wars and invasions, plagues, inquisitions and witch-hunts. I was astonished by the capacity of the people of Provence to survive.

About 700 BC, the first visitors who came, not to slaughter but to trade, were Phoenician merchants, who swapped copper, glass and cloth for smelly hides and unwanted girls. After that came the Greeks, who settled in Mes-Salya (Marseilles, to us) and brought with them all kinds of exotic trees and plants, including the olive and the vine.

Unlike the earlier Phoenicians, the Greeks refused to do business with the wild men of the hills who, they said, stank like goats. But the *Capillati*, the hairy ones, as the Romans called them, would not be ignored, and constantly attacked and raided the new Greek settlements along the coast. In due course the Romans had to come and deal with the situation, and peace reigned for some years. Then, in 102 BC, a gigantic population explosion took place in the far north, and a tidal wave of humanity came sweeping down through the plains of Western Europe. With bright blue eyes, flaming red hair and dressed in leather kilts and amber beads, they set off in their lumbering chariots and creaking oxcarts on the most enormous migration the world had ever seen, bearing down relentlessly towards the south, until eventually stopped by the sea on the shores of Provence. Thoroughly alarmed, Rome dispatched her best general to stem their progress. At all cost they had to be stopped from crossing the Alps. And as a result one of the greatest massacres of the ancient world took place in Provence.

Landing at Fos on the Rhône, Caius Marius set up camp and immediately began to train and drill his men for the great battle he was planning. Intrigued, the Barbarian hordes shuffled and lumbered around, wondering what these strange looking men were up to. In the end they grew bored and decided to push off and try their luck beyond the Alps. When the last of their cohorts had finally straggled past the Roman camp, Marius crept out with his men and discreetly followed the shambling hordes. Outnumbered by ten to one, the Romans could not afford a single wrong move. The right moment came when the rabble stopped for lunch on the banks of the River Arc. Marius gave them plenty of time to stuff themselves into a stupor. As they settled down to snooze off their beer and beef, some of the Roman legions crept to the back of the Barbarian camp to cut off any possible escape route. The remaining legions, lying low in the scrub, were holding their breath, waiting for the signal to attack. As Marius finally stood up, they charged the drowsy mob, spreading total panic throughout the camp. The men fled to their wagons, where the women split their skulls with battle-axes. The massacre raged on throughout the afternoon. As night fell, the Romans prudently retired to a small hill across the river, from which they could see the smoke of the fires below and hear the wounded tribesmen roaring and bellowing like a herd of terrified animals. The baying of their hounds and the bawling of the cattle terrorized by the afternoon onslaught added to the general chaos and pandemonium of the devastated camp.

Before dawn next day Marius ordered a second attack. A battalion of slaves was sent down to absorb the first shock. Startled out of their thick sleep, the tribesmen strapped on their leather kilts, picked up their battle-axes and scrambled blindly up the hill. Bellowing out their own names to screw up their courage, they blundered and stumbled, tripped up by their heavy shields and axes. The legions, still waiting at the back, now sprang from behind. In the uproar, hounds went mad and savaged their masters. Women with hair flying wildly in the wind snatched up their children by the feet and dashed out their brains against the wagon wheels, then plunged daggers into their own hearts. The men roped themselves to the carts by the neck and stabbed the bullocks into a wild stampede. The horror and the carnage went on till nightfall.

The plain where the battle took place has been known ever since as Pourrières (Campi Putridi) and for centuries the bleached bones of the warriors were used by the local peasants to fence in their fields. In their gratitude the people of Mes-Salya have named their sons after the Roman general ever since. Marius stands for Marseilles in the same way that everybody knows who John Bull is.

Having saved Provence from the Barbarians, the Romans were not prepared to leave the area in a hurry. From then on their aim was to subdue the entire province and bring Roman order and civilization to the region. It was Julius Caesar who finally defeated the Gauls, and Caesar Augustus who wiped out the tribes of Vence, one of the last areas to hold out against the Roman boot.

Presumably arriving on one of those boisterous days of violent mistral, Augustus named the Gallic camp Ventium, which became Vence in due course. During the four hundred years of Roman occupation, the town was a model of peace, order and spotless cleanliness, with elegant avenues, prosperous villas, fountains and temples.

When the Empire finally caved in, the hordes of Visigoths who had wiped out Rome, returned to inflict a similar fate on the thoroughly civilized Provincia Romana, determined as they were to blot out all traces of the Roman culture they so despised and hated. Then came the Burgundians, followed by Euric the Gothic warlord, an unexpectedly cultured man, by Barbarian standards anyway.

After a short pause, the most dreaded of all invaders, the Saracens, arrived in their thousands. Having crossed the Pyrenees, they ravaged the west country, until they were finally defeated at Poitiers. Unable to go further, they flooded back to Languedoc and Provence, which they were to occupy for the next six

hundred years. The Saracens controlled everything while they
ruled the province, right down to the shape of the local bread.
But it is not only the Moslem croissant – crescent – which
survives in Provence. As a race they are still there, with their
coal-black curly hair, their powerful teeth and flashing eyes,
their hot blood, their wild and passionate temperament. Intrigued
by the dynamic, aggressive vigour of the breed, I checked on
their family tree. And this led me all the way back to Abraham.
When his slave Hagar bore him a son, the boy was thrown
out of his father's camp to fend for himself in the desert. An
angel of the Lord appearing to Hagar told her that her son
would always be 'a wild donkey of a man' and would always
'live in hostility towards all his brothers'. And so the first of
the Ishmaelites started off with a chip on his shoulder, which
he handed down to all his followers. Cast out of civilization
(such as it was) they soon forgot their noble origins as
descendants of Abraham and became the terror of the desert.
Cruising through the Arabian Peninsula all the way to North
Africa, they preyed on the interminable camel caravans of the
time and ravaged settled communities. It was the Prophet
Muhammad who finally tamed them and sent them off to
conquer the world in more orderly fashion. By the time he
died in 632, Islam was firmly established at the head of a
huge empire. The Caliphs, who reigned in Damascus, ruled
most of Western Asia and the whole of North Africa.

After Rhodes, Cyprus and Crete had been converted to Islam,
General Tarek led his warriors across the Straits of Calpe in
711, to be known from then on as Gibraltar (Jebel Tarek).
The battle of Jerez landed most of Spain into his lap and was
to be ruled by Arabs for the next four hundred years. Under
their influence, mathematics, astronomy, literature, science and
medicine were taught in the new universities. Agriculture, industry and architecture were developed, and Spain became
the most civilized country of the age. Through art in all its
forms, this Oriental culture blossomed with dazzling brilliance
at a time when the rest of Europe was stumbling through the
Dark Ages, in the throes of fear, ignorance and superstition.
With all the sophisticated learning and enlightenment of Spain
under Islam, the behaviour of the Saracen conquerors in
Languedoc, Provence and Italy is hard to understand. Why
they should have regarded these lands as fit only to raid,
sack and plunder is a mystery.

The little island of St Honorat and its monastic community in the Bay of Cannes were the heart of scholarship and erudition, as well as a centre of holiness and devotion during the time of Spain's highest prestige and splendour. There, all the classical learning and culture to have survived barbarian invasions was salvaged and preserved in the monastery. St Patrick, who had been kidnapped as a child, spent several years there in prayer, study and meditation, at the end of which he sailed to Ireland to convert his ex-captors. But the idyllic life of the monastery was not to last much longer. Bishop Porchaire, who was abbot at the time calamity struck, was given a chance to save his life. But he turned it down and chose martyrdom instead. A week ahead of time an angel had appeared and warned him of a Saracen invasion already on the way and making for St Honorat. With the help of his monks he buried the monastic treasure in various parts of the island and dispatched the novices to Italy. Then he began to prepare for death.

When the Moorish sails appeared on the horizon, 505 monks, all dressed in white, headed by the abbot carrying the Cross, advanced in orderly procession to meet the enemy. Two of them decided to slip away when the carnage began. From a cave still known as Baumo de l'Abbat, to which the two monks discreetly withdrew, they saw the souls of their massacred fellow monks sailing up to Heaven in great glory. One of the refugees was so moved by the spectacle that he rushed back into the mêlée to meet his death with the others. And that was the end of St Honorat's greatest glory.

Provence was growing weary of this never-ending menace. Around the beginning of the tenth century one of the Barons, a resolute and outstanding man named William, decided to take the matter in hand. Persuading the Lords of eastern Provence to join him, they all set off together to dislodge the Saracens from their mountain hideouts. By 962, William, now known as the Liberator, flushed them out of La Garde-Freinet, their capital, and many other coastal strongholds as well. But this wasn't the end of the problem. Although they no longer lived on the spot, the Saracens still swarmed over to raid, burn and plunder the coastal villages. The last pirate landing recorded on the Riviera was in Cannes in 1835. For a short period the Knights Templars took over the defence of the coast. But after they were eliminated by the

King of France, the raids began again, as lethal as ever.

In the end, the answer to all these centuries of invasions, hit-and-run raids and massacres, was feudalism. Under this new arrangement, it was the peasants who came in for the worst part of the deal.

As serfs, they were completely at the mercy of the Barons and the Church, in exchange for protection during invasions. If ever one of these great lords was captured in battle, it was the people of the village who had to find the ransom. They were also expected to produce dowries for his daughters and to house and feed the troops of visiting grandees. A special tax was raised when the Baron was married and also at the birth of his children. His votive offerings, wars and pilgrimages were all paid for by the serfs. Then came the Church, demanding one-tenth of whatever was left over. It was a hard life for the villeins.

The man who really established feudalism in Provence as a going concern was Romeo de Villeneuve, in whose château in Vence the new public library had recently been opened. As the senior Baron among the Lords of Vence and its surroundings, Seigneur Romeo de Villeneuve was engaged by Raymond Béranger, the new Count of Provence, as his Chancellor of the Exchequer. Romeo was not only a powerful man but an astute negotiator as well. The Count was the proud father of four daughters, a rather doubtful blessing in the Middle Ages, particularly when not well endowed financially. But in spite of such a serious drawback, Romeo managed to net the most desirable husbands available for the entire quartet. Margaret, the eldest, was assigned to the King of France, the holy Louis IX. Henry III of England received the second. Next came Sancia who went to Richard, Duke of Cornwall, later to become Emperor of Germany, and Beatrice, the most attractive of them all, was married off to the French King's brother, Charles of Anjou. This move, actually engineered by the Dowager Queen of France, was a perfidious coup. By acquiring one of the Count's offspring as her daughter-in-law, she effectively reduced Provence to a mere fief of Anjou. And from that moment on, the independence of Provence began to crumble. Many of the southern towns resisted the loss of their freedom. But Charles of Anjou, probably with French help, scooped them up, one after the other, until all resistance had come to an end.

CHAPTER 4

The Many Faces of Spring

Aɴᴅ now it was more than time to get back to real work in the garden, where the early February rains and the increasing heat of the sun had caused a vegetable explosion of cosmic proportions. Electric saws and axes could be heard whirring and chopping away all day long from end to end of the garden. Even the birds found it hard to drown the man-made racket we produced.

One fine morning in early spring I got a telephone call from my accountant in London. 'I have a young client who must leave England within forty-eight hours for tax reasons. I know you have a big house. Will you take her in for the time being? It will give her a chance to look around and find her feet.'

A bit dazed I said, 'Yes, why not? Send her over.' And then, slightly worried, I broke the news to the family.

'Good idea. It will be a treat to have a young face around the place,' they all said, with variations.

So this dazzling young blonde came to join our ranks and inject some youthful blood into our middle-aged community. The first thing she did was take a long look at the garden. Her conclusion was: 'It's flowers that are needed.' As the only one among us who knew anything about gardening, she could coax whatever she wanted out of the ground. Whereas we were all chopping, slicing, uprooting, she actually began to grow things. The geraniums she put in around the house were soon blooming like the Chelsea Flower Show. To us old bumblers she seemed incredibly efficient, a kind of youthful prodigy. She had already written a book and was in charge of her family's entire fortune. Her financial advisers flew out from England to discuss business matters with her. All of which she took in her stride, as if it was the most normal thing in the world. As a rich young woman, she could have made a terrible fuss about the general discomfort and terrible shabbiness of the house. But there was never a word of complaint. She took to our rustic way of life, and our even more rustic wine, with gusto.

In spite of all his withering remarks, David managed to produce a miracle after all. In due course, a charming German couple turned up to occupy the west flat.

The morning after their arrival we knocked off work early. Our confidence had been destroyed by all the snubs and sneers, and we huddled round the garden table with our usual bottles, waiting miserably for the first complaint. Sure enough, our new tenant was ready with it. Nervously sinking our wine, we watched him advance towards us.

'Those frogs,' he said in an aggrieved voice, pointing at the fishpond behind us, 'they cry all night. Terrible noise. All night they cry and cry. What can we do?'

'Eat them,' I said, with immense relief. 'That's what people here do. They eat them.'

This was taken as a great joke, and we heard no more about the crying frogs. And in spite of them our Germans must have managed to get *some* sleep, as they were to return for another fortnight the following year.

They were followed by another Teutonic family, this time with a couple of children, who arrived to occupy the same flat. As they were settling in, Charles, who happened to be chugging past their open door with the mower, caught sight of mother and small daughters crawling about on hands and knees in the kitchen, looking for dust. Perhaps that was what David meant when he said his tenants were 'very particular'. Amazingly, they didn't seem to find any. At any rate, there were no complaints, and their fortnight passed off peacefully. The south flat, mercifully as it turned out, was still empty.

Carefree and light-hearted I set off to Monte Carlo for a few days. As the lunch hour in France is an irrevocably immovable feast, you can always be sure of a clear run through Nice from 12 noon till 3 p.m., instead of the usual stop–go crawl in bottom gear you have to endure at any other time of the day.

Once past the pompous war memorial at the foot of the

old fort, there are no more hold-ups of any kind. From then on all the way to Monte Carlo is one long stretch of cascading plumbago, flaming bougainvillaea and frothy sky-blue jacaranda. The sea on the right is dotted with the sails of small pleasure boats and hefty fishing tubs hauling in their lobster pots.

In Monte Carlo I was selling one flat and buying another, with various headaches involving a couple of house agents who were at daggers drawn. But all went well. In the masterful hands of Maître Rey, top lawyer in Monte Carlo, who conducted both operations in one session, the transaction was over in record time and the hostile agents behaved like lambs. Maître Rey handed over the keys, and off I went at top speed to take possession of my new quarters.

Though bare and empty and in need of new paint, the flat was still a dream come true. The view over the sea stretched from the Italian Riviera in the east, all the way round as far as Nice, way off to the right. A row of french windows opened on to a long balcony overlooking the harbour below and its fleet of millionaires' yachts and, behind them, the Rock of Monaco-Ville, with the famous sea museum at one end and Prince Rainier's palace at the other. Flopping down on to the balcony's cold tiles I stared round, soaking up the view in a state of undiluted bliss.

Portus Monoeci, as it was known to the Romans, was full of dinghies busily skimming in and out, leaving long white curves in the water as they swung round the lighthouse on their way to lunch in Nice, Cannes or Juan-les-Pins. Lined up along the jetty, the larger yachts and launches stood guard opposite the yacht club. Small though the harbour is, it can accommodate up to 150 boats all the same. *La Belle Simone*, moored outside the Onassis office, was pretty well a fixture, as her owner, in those days, lived on board. *Atlantis*, the largest yacht in the world, which belonged to Niarchos, was 116 metres long, with a top speed of 22 knots, and could stay out at sea for 90 days, with 70 passengers on board without having to stop for supplies. And I was glad to see that staunch old *Calypso*, the floating research vessel in which Captain Cousteau explores the sea-world of the planet, was there as well.

But how different it all was from my childhood days, when only rowing boats paddled about in the harbour, loaded with fishing nets and lobster pots, a lantern at the helm, a boy battling with the oars, and all of it creaking and squeaking in the mellow evening light. In those days Monte Carlo was a graceful curve of private villas hugging the shore around the bay. Sixty years later, it is an imposing mini Manhattan, with luxury high-rise flats, a booming economy, foreign banks and businesses accumulating fortunes in the tax-free haven of Monaco.

Established on their Rock since the early Middle Ages, the Grimaldis are the oldest reigning family ever to have ruled in the western world. During the Middle Ages they were constantly at war, usually joining another army, lending a hand, as when they fought with William the Liberator against Moorish invasions. After the destruction of Les Baux by Cardinal Richelieu, the French King handed over the ruin and the title to the Grimaldis in return for their constant military help in times of trouble.

Originally financed by a toll on coastal shipping and tax raised in Menton and Roquebrune, both of which belonged to Monaco, the little state was almost bankrupt when these two settlements became independent in 1848. It was then that Prince Florestan decided to build up Monaco into a resort. A gaming house and bathing establishment were planned, several entrepreneurs tried and failed, until François Blanc was approached.

Monsieur Blanc, who had made a fortune from a casino he had launched in Bad Homburg in 1843, took on Monaco as his next project and officially contracted to set up a Société des Bains de Mer, a casino and the Cercle des Etrangers in Monaco. Soon a new town had sprung up out of the stony old plateau, surrounded by large hotels, over a hundred villas, streets, fountains and exotic gardens. *Le Figaro* newspaper gave it a rousing launch, but the casino only took off in a big way when the Prince allowed the Nice–Genoa railway to run through his state. Monte Carlo was soon so prosperous that all taxation could be, and was, cancelled.

Enormous fortunes were made during that first phenomenal year. The abolition of the second zero at roulette was acclaimed all over Europe, and caused a rush of hopeful royals and aristocrats into Monte Carlo, including the Prince of Wales himself, the Emperor and Empress of Austria, the King of the Belgians and a clutch of Russian Grand Dukes.

A theatre and an opera house were built within the Casino building, and a succession of brilliant productions took place. Apart from plays, concerts and operas, Diaghilev brought his

Russian ballets with Nijinsky, Pavlova, Karsavina, Danilova and many others. Stage sets were painted by Picasso, Miró, Max Ernst. After the First World War, Lifar picked up the thread again with his 'Nouveaux Ballets', and the tradition was kept going, with Maurice Béjart at the head of the 'Ballets du 20ᵉ Siecle'.

But it was time to stop day-dreaming on my balcony and get ready for the evening. The Irish Library was holding a cocktail party at the Hotel de Paris for the launch of the twelfth International James Joyce Symposium.

Founded by Prince Rainier in 1984, the Princess Grace Irish Library was the main cultural centre of the Principality. Quite close to the palace, the building contains Princess Grace's personal collection of books and musical scores, mostly of Irish folk-songs. The library was run by a professor, who had set up the entire project from its very beginning. It was he who organized the annual seminars, the meetings, lectures on Irish literature, concerts, films and exhibitions all through the year. The huge Joyce Symposium, which took place in June 1990 and which was masterminded by the professor, had established the Monte Carlo Irish Library as *the* centre for James Joyce and all Irish studies.

That evening the party at the Hotel de Paris was an occasion for *tout Monaco* to turn up, after which the entire company drifted off to the Yacht Club for dinner.

Next day the proceedings started at 9 a.m. with a lecture by Anthony Burgess, himself a resident of Monte Carlo. And until the end of the convention, the daily programme seldom ended before midnight. The overseas guests turned up for all the lectures, which were well attended by the local residents as well. Altogether it was a triumph for the Irish Library, and its members were duly gratified.

At the end of the week, early on Saturday morning, I drove back to Vence. And there I was in for a shock. As I chugged up the drive, something unusual seemed to be going on. A curious brown liquid was trickling down the front steps of the south flat. With a pang of alarm I shot out of the car.

In the hall Anne stood with her jeans stuffed into her gum-boots and that awful look of desolation on her face that I knew so well. 'It's spouting out of the loo like a geyser every time they pull the plug in the west flat,' she bleated, almost in tears. 'There it goes again. Come and have a look.'

'Certainly not. Come out of there at once,' I yelled.

At this point David's car came sweeping up the drive. 'Hullo, hullo, hullo, how is everything going?' he piped cheerily as he tripped up to the front door. There he stopped dead in his tracks. 'My Gawd!' he neighed, clapping a hand over his nose. 'My poor darlings . . . I wish I could help you, but there's nothing, absolutely nothing I can do for you.' And with that he skipped back into his car and was gone.

'Come out of there, for heaven's sake,' I moaned as Anne stood rooted to the spot in a trance. 'I'll go and get the village pump right away.' And off I sped to the town hall to request the loan of the 'Film Star', as it was affectionately known to the locals.

This malodorous appliance was frequently seen parked here and there in the narrow streets of Vence, hard at work unblocking drains, sucking out cesspits and generally making itself useful. But the sanitation officer flatly refused to help. 'Our pump is overworked already. We can't spare it for a moment. This is your problem, not mine.'

'Do you realize that the plague could break out any minute? The whole of Vence could be wiped out in a matter of hours.'

'Madame, this is nothing to do with me. Find your own solution, and let me get on with my work,' he said coldly.

So off I galloped through the streets, calling on every plumber in town. Each one said firmly that 'it wasn't his province'. Once the situation was out of control, as was only too obvious in our case, there was nothing they could do.

'Whose job is it, then?' I asked in despair.

'The sanitary engineers. Go and see them. They'll help you.'

Gone full circle, I was back where I started.

At this point Charles suddenly appeared in the square, obviously looking for me. 'Let's go and have a glass of beer,' he said.

'I need something a lot stronger than that,' I groaned. We hurried over to the Régence.

'What about Arduin?' he asked.

'Yes, what about him?'

'He mended the roof. He's coped with the plumbing already. He can do anything. He might have a pump . . .'

'Ah, brilliant!' I whooped, and shot across the road under the nose of a screaming, swearing taxi. Miraculously, the public telephone was working and Arduin was at home. And, yes, he knew of a private pump which went in for this kind of business. He would contact the owner and bring both up to Mas Mistral the moment they were available.

Within a couple of hours the machine was installed and hard at work. Almost at once it became perfectly obvious that the wistaria roots were at the heart of the matter. Already having burst through the tiles of the hall, they had now sneaked into the waste pipes as well, to feed on their contents. Fattened up by all these nourishing juices, they had blocked the drains solid with their exuberant growth. Getting down to it with every chopper we could find, we attacked the great slimy, stinking coils and pulverized them. We went on hacking away until they looked as if they could never grow again.

Finally it was all cleaned up, hosed down, disinfected, sprayed and smelling like a tart's boudoir. But the real miracle was that somehow we had managed the entire operation in total secrecy, while the people in the west wing went on cheerfully pulling their plug without ever suspecting a thing.

David, who was surpassing himself in finding us a constant flow of customers, announced that a new lot were arriving the next day. And when they turned up to occupy the now fresh and fragrant flat, they were the last thing we expected – a bouncing family of nudists . . .

They jogged around the garden, lay in the grass to sunbathe and displayed an impressive collection of glowing bums for several days.

Assuming we were also tenants, they joined us before lunch to practise their English. Faithful to their creed they brought their own carrot and celery juice, and we could not even persuade them to taste our wine. As vegetarians they concocted all kinds of strange-looking mock meat dishes, which they generously offered to share with us. Charles and Pierre turned them down with cries of horror, while Anne and I declined more politely. Quite unperturbed, they trotted round to the west flat with their unwanted offerings. As they left, Charles informed their retreating backsides that 'Fleisch ist das beste gemüse', at which they roared with laughter. By the time they left they were looking incredibly fit and tanned. Even their bottoms were like saddle leather.

Once their car was packed, one of the women, by then dressed for the trip and looking strangely unfamiliar, asked to borrow a garden fork. With this she rooted up the geraniums

Ariane had so recently put in, 'To see if they will grow in Berlin', she said to me with a wink and still having no idea we were the owners. Only too glad that it had all gone so well, I returned her wink and let her carry off our blooming treasures without a word.

That afternoon David warned us to be ready for new recruits within twenty-four hours.

The next day, sitting round our lunch-time bottles, we waited for the next contingent to appear. And there it was, a large German car coming slowly up the drive. Stopping in front of the house, it remained there for a couple of minutes, then gathered itself up and sped off again down the central drive. Nobody had even got out of the car.

Could the house really be so ghastly, even from outside, we wondered, thoroughly crestfallen. To us it looked magnificent: the wistaria growing again, of course, but trimmed well back, the gleaming, newly painted blue shutters and a wall of pink geraniums climbing to the first floor, looping gracefully over the balcony. And all round bloomed the Judas trees, the jasmine and syringa, while the cherry trees were covered with ripening fruit. What more could anybody want? If they had gone inside and suffered from shock at our colour scheme, or my South Seas mural, or the kitchen pipes, we could have understood and even sympathized. But fleeing like that, after a few seconds . . . We were stunned.

In our distress we rang up David. 'Oh dear,' he said. 'I told you it was a sad place.'

'But they didn't even get out of the car!'

He had to admit it sounded fishy. 'We'll let sleeping dogs lie,' he said with his usual caution.

Next day the master of the family marched up the drive, stared at the house, picked up his German newspaper left by the postman and stalked off down the drive again. For the next fortnight, punctually at 10 a.m. he turned up every day, performed the same ritual and disappeared.

David, who came round to watch with us, was equally baffled. 'You can be sure he'll claim his rent back when he gets home,' he said. 'You'll have to pay up, dears. I don't want any trouble.'

But we never heard a word from him, either when he returned to Germany or since. The whole affair has remained a complete mystery to this day.

CHAPTER 5

Vence Then and Now

MEANWHILE we carried on with our endless labours in the garden. The old grassmower, tethered to Charles's twitching arms now the colour of mahogany, kicked and bucked its way up and down the terraces. From dawn to dusk Pierre, wielding his ferocious Japanese scythe and up to his neck in brambles, sliced, slashed and hacked away at the scrub. His progress could be followed by the small cloud of fumes hovering over his head as he went about his business. Anne never stopped cooking, weeding, ironing and restoring old furniture.

The lower terraces, which had fallen to my lot, could not be put off any longer. I knew from memory that an ancient orchard lurked somewhere beneath all that rampaging jungle. My job was to liberate the fruit trees from its stranglehold.

Anxious at the thought of the horrors ahead, I set off down the central drive. Only too soon I was face to face with the enemy – a solid wall of impenetrable vegetation.

Hurling my billhook at it with all the strength I could muster, I – was – slowly – lifted – off – my – feet. Then, rather more smartly, I crashed face forward into the murderous thorns. This took a good deal of sorting out. After mopping up the blood and getting my breath back, there was nothing for it but to wade right into it once more. With rather less *élan* this time, I hacked to right and left, hauling the spiky vines down from their tangled canopy. A couple of magpies floated up with furious quarks, and dived at my face. Bees and wasps wafted around in clouds. Millions of midges shimmered at eye level. I plugged on. By the end of the day the results were meagre. One scrawny cherry tree stood free. And my

left leg was very sore. All that night it throbbed and swelled.
By the morning it was the size of a bolster. When I drove
down to a chemist in Vence, he took one look at it and said,
impressed, 'That's an adder's bite. Look at the little fang holes.
I'm afraid there's nothing I can do. You'll have to go and see
a doctor.'

'Well, well,' said the medic when I finally managed to
hobble round to his surgery. 'I haven't seen one of those
here before. Lucky you're not a dog or a donkey. You'd be
dead by now.'

'What's going to happen?' I asked, with visions of the leg
slowly rotting away and dropping off.

'If you keep quite still, it won't spread above the knee. But
you'll be in trouble if the poison gets into the gland.'

Keeping still was no problem. I now had a cast-iron ex-
cuse, and nobody could blame me for getting down to my
books again.

The next morning the leg was still swollen enough to justify one more day of loafing. After that, as I was granted a
short break to recover from the trauma, I decided to totter
down to the village to see what was going on.

When I reached the square, there was Phyllis Cahill sitting
at a table with Muriel Broad on the terrace of the Régence,
both lapping their morning drink. Muriel ran the newly opened
English Library on the first floor of the château. Her friend
Phyllis had been living in Vence for over sixty years.

'Tell me about the place in the twenties,' I said as I joined
them at their table. 'I can't remember as much as I would
like to about those days.'

'Well, I expect you remember the Rendez-Vous, don't you?'
said Phyllis.

'I certainly do. I remember my father being dragged there
under protest from time to time. What was it like?'

'It was run by an Englishman as a kind of international
meeting place for the British, American, Dutch, Danes and
what-have-you who haunted the place at that time. They all
met in one of those tall, narrow houses down by the Basse-
Fontaine.'

'Yes, I do remember the place,' I said.

'Well, for a time, the club was a great success. It was open
all day and drinks and tea were on tap at all times. People
played bridge, gossiped, read the papers and enjoyed one

another's company. The foreign artists organized new shows
of their work every fortnight, when a gala took place for
the private view. Everybody wore evening dress and danced
to an old wind-up gramophone. Of course, jeans and long
hair hadn't been thought of at the time,' Phyllis said, 'but
the artists did their best with floppy bow-ties and a look of
picturesque poverty.

'Gradually the smart people from the coast began to pat-
ronize the club, and soon it was a swinging success. Well-
known artists, including Augustus John, came up to Vence to
inspect the painters' work.

'But in spite of the club's increasing popularity, there never
seemed to be enough cash at the end of the month to pay
the bills. Quite often the rooms were in total darkness, with
a few candles stuck here and there in wine bottles. The elec-
tricity bill had been unpaid for too long,' said Phyllis, chortling
at the memory.

Then one day the local bailiff was spotted in the hall, counting
the heads as they came in. At the end of the evening he
rushed to the till and scooped up all the takings. And then
the awful truth came out. Every night after the last guest had
left, the manager would rush off to the casino in Nice and
squander the evening's profits. Three times the richer members set him up again and restocked his bar, and every time
he dashed straight off to lose it all at the tables. In the end
the Rendez-Vous went bankrupt and closed its doors for the
last time, and the manager went back to England in disgrace.

'Why didn't anyone start it up again?' I asked.

'Nobody was willing to cope with the problems he had
created. But we had a lot of fun while it lasted,' Phyllis concluded.

'Did you know Frank Harris? Did he ever come up here?'

'He did. In Vence he was always known as that funny little
man with the dyed whiskers.'

'And did he dye his hair as well?'

'Of course. He would have been completely white otherwise, and that wasn't the image he wanted to project.'

'Whatever brought him up to Vence?'

'He and Nellie used to come and visit Auntie, who always
welcomed foreigners, especially if they were well known.'

Auntie, an ex-journalist, had lived in Vence even longer
than Phyllis. She ran a pottery-cum-teashop and a kind of
children's club to which we were taken for dancing lessons

in our extreme youth. She was a mine of information about life in the little town in the old days.

'Auntie was a great name collector,' Phyllis went on. 'Her self-appointed task was to dole out tea and cakes, gossip and endless stories to her guests. And after that we all trooped off to the Rendez-Vous.'

'Did the Harrises bring their entourage with them?'

'I'm afraid they didn't have much of an entourage. They usually arrived on their own and invariably came all the way from Nice by taxi, even though he was chronically short of cash. But in spite of that, and whatever people may say, he was tremendously generous to those who were down on their luck. When Oscar Wilde came over after they let him out of prison, Frank helped him as much as he could.'

'Why was he so short of cash?' I asked. 'I thought he was such a successful newspaper editor.'

'Oh yes, he stormed his way through quite a few papers and magazines in London. Everything he had a hand in turned to disaster sooner or later.'

Towards the end of the last century Harris spent a great deal of time on the Riviera in the wake of the Prince of Wales, who was much amused by his 'naughty stories'.

'"You can do anything you like", the Prince used to say, "as long as you don't frighten the horses." But the trouble with Harris was that he always went out of his way to frighten the horses. So, as was bound to happen, he ruffled the Prince of Wales's feathers and lost HRH's friendship,' Phyllis said. 'Princess Alice of Monaco, who met him in 1890, was genuinely devoted to him and was anxious to help him in any way she could.'

Princess Alice's husband, Prince Albert, had also been well disposed at the beginning. They went shooting together, and Harris taught him to ride a bicycle. But Frank could not help pushing things too far. He announced that he wanted to take over the Casino and turn it into a sporting club. Prince Albert knew only too well that his wild friend was no businessman. As expected, the giddy scheme came to nothing. A contract was signed with the far more reliable Camille Blanc, and Harris, wild with rage, screamed that he had been betrayed. And one more of his grand friends was lost to his cause.

The next venture was a restaurant by the sea at Eze, where Cap Estel now stands. Then came the Palace Hotel in Monte

Carlo, on which he spent somebody else's fortune. Prince Albert who obviously knew what was coming, would not allow Princess Alice to visit the restaurant or launch the hotel. Both projects were a total failure.

'As it turned out,' said Phyllis, 'neither venture had been registered according to legal requirements, so they couldn't even open up for business. The restaurant had to be sold, and the hotel was made bankrupt. Confusion was total. Harris dropped everything and fled to London.'

Always an obsessive female hunter, he still regarded himself as God's gift to women. In spite of his squat and graceless looks, he made a heavy pass at almost every female he met.

'How did they take it?' I asked.

'Many fell for it, but I think they were more stunned by the onslaught than taken in by the flattery. Poor Nellie had a terrible time with him,' Phyllis went on.

His American followers confused Harris still more by comparing him to Christ, with the difference that his approach was through the flesh, instead of the spirit. And so, by the time he was seventy, poor old Frank really believed he was the Messiah. It was then that he conferred the honour of marriage upon Nellie, who had already been living with him for many years. And although he was always wildly unfaithful to her, she stayed with him till the end of his life. His health and his temper, never very good, grew worse as time went by. Asthma and bronchitis had plagued him for years. Terrible fits of hiccups, no doubt due to the stomach pump which he used constantly, did not improve matters.

The lack of funds was a constant worry. Nellie had to pawn her jewellery and the family silver. She was often in despair, especially when Frank's old friends turned up for a loan, which he invariably produced. But others, like Bernard Shaw and Charlie Chaplin, tried to help, a boost to their morale. And then there were the extravagant taxi trips to Vence, the tea parties in Auntie's shop and the art shows at the Rendez-Vous. These gala evenings with dancing to the old gramophone manned by the taxi driver, with the help of a bottle of wine, ended up with eggs and bacon and Champagne in the early hours of the morning.

'After this, Frank and Nellie set off down the hill on their uncertain course, piloted by a very tipsy taxi driver,' Phyllis concluded.

As she finished her story, Charles appeared in the square, 'Let's go and find Ariane,' he said. 'She can give us a lift home,'

'Where is she? I haven't seen her.'

'Buying plants in the market to make up for the ones the nudists nicked before they left.'

On the church square the market was in full swing, with people swarming in all directions. Vans, lorries, handcarts, three-wheelers, motorbikes were grinding into gear, shoving, backing and hurling insults. 'Crétin, imbécile, abruti, espèce de con,' they growled and hissed as they crashed and banged into one another's vehicles.

Ariane had soon acquired a car of her own. Unlike the rest of us, who dutifully left our old bangers in the car park, she always drove right into the centre of the old town, where even cats and dogs find it hard to navigate.

As she suddenly emerged from the corner bistro, her bright hair stood on end all round her head and her eyes blazed. 'Stinking rotters,' she snarled, breathing fire.

Charles blinked at her. 'What on earth were you doing in there?'

'Telling those louts to move their cars. They've hemmed me in. But they're all glued to their television football, and they absolutely refused to budge.'

'Come on, let's get our plants,' Charles said.

Under the arch of the Bishop's palace, Madame Roux had her stand. Her flowers, grown in her own greenhouses further up the valley, were the best in the market. Robust and vigorous, they last for years. Madame Roux is a well-known character in Vence, quite different from the local people in looks, temperament and every possible way. With her thin, narrow face and arched profile, she has the aristocratic features of a Roman coin. Way back in the heart of the Alps is the small village where she was born. Bred in those harsh surroundings, she was used to hard work and discipline. Unfortunately, as she told me one day, when she was too young to know better, she had married a Southerner, a good-for-nothing who drank away the money she earned with her plants. But there was no bitterness in her voice. She simply said, 'My husband is a rotter,' as she might have announced that he was a plumber or a bell-ringer. With her usual efficient and courteous manner, she wrapped up our geraniums in newspaper, and we loaded them into the back of Ariane's now liberated car. Then off we set, wasting no more time, back to Mas Mistral for lunch.

When I told Anne about the Rendez-Vous stories I had just heard, she looked thoughtful. 'Hang on,' she said. 'I think there's something that might interest you.' And she dashed off into the house. Half an hour later she was back, waving a small book over her head. 'Here you are. I found it in the attic. Have a look at it.'

Vence, Immortal Village, written in the twenties by the American author Donald Culross Peattie, the story of the little town going back to the days of Ligurian mud huts, is the most comprehensive and delightful history of Vence that I have ever read. It is, moreover, still in print. Morris Philipson, present owner of Chicago University Press, which originally published Peattie's book all those years ago, sent me a copy of a new edition of it, which he had recently brought out.

Curious about what had happened in Vence after Peattie finished his book and returned to the United States, I decided to go and find out right away. Next day, hoping to see Phyllis in the square, I made straight for the Régence, where she was sitting with her paper and her wine as usual. Obligingly, she put *Nice-Matin* away when I explained what I was after.

'Did you ever meet Peattie?' I asked.

'No, he left just before I arrived, but of course I've read his book.'

'And is that how you remember the village at the time?'

'Oh, absolutely. But there is one side of life in those days which he doesn't mention.'

'And what was that?'

'Well, perhaps he never met them, but there were already quite a few foreigners about, attracted by the unpretentious artlessness of the place. And, of course, the low cost of living. You could get along very well on a couple of pounds a week.'

'But,' she went on, 'it was from Auntie that I heard all about Vence in the first place. I met her in England, and she talked me into coming over on a visit.' Auntie's pottery shop in the square behind the château was still a bustling social centre after the Second World War.

'I came, I saw, I was conquered,' Phyllis told me. 'Within a few days Vence was in my blood. And here I am, over sixty years later, and still enjoying every second of the day.' She knew all the local people, and the foreign eccentrics as well. 'There was a handful of impecunious painters, a nudist colony and several writers.' A troup of Scandinavian dancers performed by moonlight under the plane trees in the square. A bunch of vegetarians lived in a commune up in the hills. Nowadays all these characters would be described as hippies. At the time they were labelled foreign atheists, people who never went to Mass on Sunday.

Auntie, who had known various literary celebrities in London, always entertained them when they came to Vence, doing her best to lionize them. 'My chief recollection of Norman Douglas was of him dodging her,' Phyllis said. She remembered him slinking furtively through the back streets. 'Is the old girl in her lair?' he would ask. On being told she was waiting for him at Tony's bar (now Henry's), he nipped off to the Cave Bleue to join his cronies. As he came up to Vence to avoid the summer crowds on the coast, all he wanted was peace and tranquillity.

Phyllis never met D. H. Lawrence, but she came to know Frieda quite well after he died. 'It was Auntie, of course, who told Frieda about me. She asked me to type her husband's love letters and two or three one-act plays that she wanted to take to the States.'

The hundredth anniversary of Lawrence's birth was celebrated in 1985 in Eastwood, where he was born. At the same time a blue plaque was placed more or less on the spot where he died in Vence in 1930, in the Villa Robermont, adjoining our land. As the villa had since then been pulled down, the plaque had to be screwed on to one of the gateposts of the new flats that had taken its place. Hardly an impressive monument but the best that could be done in the circumstances. The town councillors took the trouble to be present. Phyllis, Muriel and I were there, and the Mayor made an appropriate speech. 'A simple ceremony,' Muriel concluded, 'but it was nice of them to do it.'

The reason I remember the day Lawrence arrived in Vence, 6 February 1930, is because of the flood. My mother and I, engrossed in our books in the drawing room at Mas Mistral, were totally oblivious of what was going on around us. Sitting on our feet on account of the draughts, we were completely unaware of the storm and the cataracts of water cascading through the house. It was only when a mat came waltzing past on the swirling stream that I jolted back to consciousness.

We did not know it at the time, but at that very moment Lawrence was moving into the sanatorium at the top of our garden. Suffering from tuberculosis since 1911, he had always refused to face the problem. After teaming up with Frieda, they both landed at Bandol, where Katherine Mansfield had already brought her wasted lungs. Andrew Morland, a doctor who looked after some of the Bloomsbury Group and had managed to cure Mark Gertler of the same complaint, was going to the Riviera for a holiday. On hearing this, Gertler begged him to go and see Lawrence. The visit duly took place, and the patient was found to be weak, fragile and altogether in very poor shape. He needed professional attention, which could not be laid on at home. Much against his will he was persuaded by Morland to move to Ad Astra, the tuberculosis sanatorium a few hundred yards up the hill.

In those days it was thought beneficial for the afflicted to lie in full sunshine on the sanatorium's terraces. We now know that this treatment considerably hastened their demise.

Lawrence, who was thoroughly miserable in such surroundings, had visits from various friends who climbed up the hill in the filthy winter weather to see him. H. G. Wells brought him books. The Aga Khan offered to give him a show of his paintings, and the canvases duly arrived on Auntie's doorstep in Vence. His devoted friends Aldous and Maria Huxley turned up just as he decided to leave Ad Astra. Frieda had been persuaded to rent Villa Robermont and he moved to it on 1 March. With his friends around him he felt much happier. But he could eat nothing, and there was no sleep that night. The next day was worse. He asked for morphia, after which he was more comfortable. He died peacefully that night at ten o'clock.

The funeral was very plain. There was no ceremony. The Huxleys were there, as well as Frieda's daughter, Barbara Weekly and, of course, Auntie. They threw great branches of flowering mimosa on the coffin, and that was the last act in the life of D. H. Lawrence.

Frieda stayed on at Robermont, where John Middleton Murry came to cheer her up, and they resumed their previous affair. It was at this point that Phyllis Cahill was recruited to type Lawrence's letters to Frieda.

After Frieda gave up Robermont, she went off to Italy to persuade one of her ex-lovers to go to New Mexico with her. Once there they were married, they settled down at Taos, where she proceeded to build a shrine to Lawrence, then decided to have his remains brought over from Vence. Much against his will, her new husband was dispatched to collect them.

For some reason, it was Auntie who applied for the exhumation permit. She reported later that, when the coffin was opened, the body was in a state of perfect preservation, but a few minutes later there was nothing but dust and bones. As a good journalist, she took photographs before and after. These, unfortunately, disappeared at her death.

Some time later she rescued the tombstone from oblivion, and stowed it away under the sink in her kitchen. Allsebrook Ross Williamson, who stayed with my parents in Vence after the last war, told me that he often saw it in her teashop. Others spotted it on the balcony, also by the front door. It was obviously shunted around whenever it got in the way.

When she returned to England, Auntie tried to sell the tombstone to Professor Vivian de Sola Pinto for £200, a sum she probably needed badly at the time. But she died before the deal could go through, and the owner of her hotel then presented it to Professor Pinto, who sent it to Eastwood. And there it is to this day. Designed by Dominique Matteucci, it is decorated with a sphinx in brightly coloured pebbles. An interesting, if not a very distinguished monument.

CHAPTER 6

City of the Popes

AFTER a quick visit to London, Charles and I were on our way back to the South, bumping along minor patched-up roads through the immensity of the French countryside. It had been my own idea, not exactly encouraged by Charles, to visit the Palace of the Popes on the way and spend a night in Avignon. Feeling responsible for the situation, I was much relieved to find a room in the main hotel in the heart of the medieval city *and* space for the car, almost unheard of in Avignon.

Emerging from the dark, narrow streets of the old town, we stood bemused. There, across the huge paved square, stood the colossal fortress of the Popes, with its formidable walls and towers all glowing like Normandy butter in the late afternoon sunshine. Leaning against the palace wall, a lone figure piped a mournful tune. The sound, in the deserted square, was eerie.

Philip the Fair, King of France, had installed the first Pope in Avignon to control the power of the Templar Knights, who had the full backing of the Roman pontiff. As Philip was planning to exterminate the Order of the Temple and requisition its funds for his own purposes, this was his solution to bypassing the Vatican's authority in the matter.

Started by Benedict XII in 1334, the enormous complex of palace and citadel was enlarged by his successor when he took over the massive pile in 1342. As an infinitely cultured and sophisticated man, great prince of the Church and patron of the arts, Clement VI's own construction is far more elegant and attractive than the severe old dungeon next door. Built on the living rock, it is indestructible.

As we approached the entrance, the sun disappeared and the rain, which had been bucketing down on and off throughout

the day, started to crash out of the sky again, and was soon
roaring down the enormous medieval waterspouts. As guides
assembled their busloads of tourists, we pushed through them
into the huge bare audience hall and the consistory beyond,
where kings and ambassadors were received with great pomp
and new saints were proclaimed.

Nowadays there are only five Gobelin tapestries hanging in
the banqueting hall. Those which escaped looting during the
Revolution went up in flames in various fires. But at the height
of its glory, under the reign of Pope Clement VI, the walls
and ceilings of the palace were covered with frescos, banners, tapestries, coats of arms, heraldic shields and all kinds
of other trophies.

'Every meal was a banquet in itself,' I heard a guide proclaim.
'The cardinals had to sit back to back in special stalls so as
not to put one another off their food with their personal
eating habits. They rummaged about in the dishes with their
fingers and dripped fat all over the tablecloth,' he prattled on.

The feast to celebrate Clement VI's coronation is still remembered in Avignon to this day. On that occasion five thousand
carcases of roast oxen, sheep, calves, deer, were consumed
by the guests. Sixty-nine tons of bacon were used to lard all
the plump and shapely breasts of hundreds of roast swans,
quail, peacocks and capercaillie.

At another party thrown in the Pope's honour by his trusty
cardinals, the twenty-seven courses included a huge pie containing a live deer and its harem, a wild boar bristling with
rage and fury and a rush of hares and rabbits. This makes
the nursery rhyme of four-and-twenty blackbirds baked in a
pie seem rather small beer. The wine, best Châteauneuf du
Pape, flowed from a fountain in the shape of a clocktower,
round which flocks of pheasants, peacocks and partridges pecked
on an emerald lawn of real growing grass. Herons stalked
about and flights of thrushes zoomed in and out among them
and crashed, blind drunk, into the wine fountain. Nobody throws
parties like this in Avignon any more.

By the time Clement VI became Pope, the town had grown
into a bustling tourist centre, as well as a hive of creative
activity. The court of that most civilized of pontiffs was soon
a meeting place for men of letters, painters, princes, noblemen
and ambassadors from all over Europe. They flocked to the
papal court to pay their respects to His Holiness, to see who

else was there and, of course, to be seen themselves. Life in
Avignon, the 'Tinkling Town', was brilliant, dazzling, ebullient.
The Court welcomed every new idea and all the latest fash-
ions with the greatest enthusiasm. The Renaissance, with all
its robust vigour, was soon established and flourishing in the
new capital of Christianity. Everybody was accepted, from Jews
and Cathars to political prisoners and common criminals, as
long as they had something to offer. Merchants on their way
back from the great international fair at Beaucaire stopped off
to spend their takings in the free-and-easy, open-minded city.

The Pope's personal fortune grew and multiplied, pouring
in from wills, bequests, gifts, from the sale of bulls, pardons,
dispensations and indulgences. At his death this enormous
wealth, stowed away beneath the private apartments, included
gold and silver plate, jewellery, church apparel and mountains of bullion. Coin collecting became known as 'the Pope's
little industry'.

After Clement's death, the cardinals, locked up as usual to
elect his successor, found it very difficult to nominate anyone
else and were quite unable to come to a decision. To help
them along in their task, their rations were gradually reduced
day by day until the new incumbent was finally elected.

It was St Catherine of Siena who finally brought the
sparkling life of the town to an end. In 1377 she persuaded
Gregory II (the seventh Pope of Avignon) to return to the
Vatican, the official papal court since the days of St Peter.
His Holiness, who had no wish to leave the glittering town,
held back as long as he could. Nobody wanted him to go.
But Catherine, who saw it as her mission in life, was
determined to get him back if it was the last thing she did.
The weeping Pope was finally bundled off to Rome, and
that was the end of Avignon's days of glory, which dissolved
overnight the moment the papal court came to an end.

Further down the Rhône Valley, at the top end of Camargue,
Arles is as different from the City of the Popes as it can
possibly be. Built by Caesar, it was the capital of Provincia
Romana, the present Provence.

The most remarkable feature of the old capital of Provence
is the enormous arena with twenty thousand seats, built by
the Romans in such a way that in case of fire or earthquake
it can be evacuated in five minutes flat.

The famous Arles Museum was set up by the poet Mistral, with cash received for his Nobel prize in 1896, and it was here that the golden locks of Princess Strella of Florence found a permanent home.

And the last, but to me the most intriguing feature of all, is the graveyard of Alyscamps, the largest and best-known necropolis of the ancient world.

Since the early Renaissance, systematic plundering of the cemetery had become the custom, and town officials, monasteries and local citizens stole everything they fancied to decorate their own establishments. But in spite of these depredations, there are still a great number of handsome and elegant monuments left in the old necropolis.

Following the Roman custom of never building cemeteries within their walls, the Via Aurelia, leading out of the town, had been a pagan graveyard since early times, with the gods of the underworld watching and brooding over their own. Then came St Trophimus, who converted the old burial ground to Christianity and chased the pagan devils away to the depths of a nearby lake.

As we came to the end of the long grave-lined avenue, we reached the banks of the Rhône, where flotsam of every kind spun past on the fast-flowing stream.

'This is where corpses used to float down the river with a coin between their teeth,' said a man who had come to stand beside us. 'Anything coasting down the river will get washed up on this bank,' he went on. 'In the Middle Ages gravediggers would wait here with boathooks to haul in the corpses as they arrived. Some were tied to rafts. Others travelled in wine barrels. But the poorer ones were launched on the water in their Sunday best, with a prayer and a coin to pay for their burial.'

Those who did not come floating down the current were often strapped to specially trained horses who knew the way. Setting off along the towpath with his ghoulish rider, the horse would sometimes travel for several days, pulling in for a quick bite of oats at various staging posts along the way. Having delivered his load to the gravediggers, he would then canter back the way he had come.

Some candidates who wanted to choose their own site themselves would come and camp near the cemetery and wait for death to collect them. One worthy merchant from Lyons was told by his doctors that he had not got long to live. So, sharing out his fortune among his family, he gave a farewell party for his friends and set off on his horse with a sizeable sum in his purse. He might as well, he thought, have a good time while waiting to be gathered. The news soon spread around Arles that this gentleman who looked so prosperous was determined to enjoy himself. People flocked to his inn, offered to show him round and take him to all the merriest spots in town. The first two weeks were a riot. But instead of feeling worse as expected, his health improved more and more as the days went by. Far from dying as he was meant to, he steadily and relentlessly grew stronger and fitter and more robust.

With increasing alarm he saw that the funds he had brought with him were dwindling fast. Finally, having spent his last ducat, and living on crusts for a week or two, hoping that starvation would put an end to his problem, he had to get back on his horse and make for home. Consternation greeted him on arrival. Everyone had assumed him to be dead and safely buried in his dream graveyard. His wife had married again.

The couple took him in, but it was an impossible situation. With no money, no wife and no home, he was forced to leave his native town again. There was only one thing for him to do. Not far from Arles, perched on a rocky height and surrounded by swamps, was the mighty fortified abbey of Montmajour. So there he went, planning as a last resort to enlist in the order and become a monk. But without a dowry there was no question of joining the hierarchy. He had to enrol as a second-class novice and was put to work in the garden. The poor man not only had to dig the kitchen garden but also the graves of his brother monks.

When the end finally, came, he was laid to rest among the bones and the stones of the monastery graveyard, a far cry from the prestigious Alyscamps of his dreams so long ago.

Sic transit gloria mundi.

CHAPTER 7

Knights of the Olive

WHEN we got back from Avignon, olive time was upon us and the harvest was in full swing all over the South. Everywhere peasants were banging away at the trees with long poles and raking up mountains of olives. As our own trees had been wiped out by the great frost of 1956, there was no harvest for us to gather.

Feeling deprived and frustrated at missing one of the great symbolic rituals of Provence, I asked Vivienne Glenavy if I could help with the ceremonial in her own five-hundred-year-old grove at Le Rouret.

Vivienne, the intrepid widow of the third Baron Glenavy, alias Patrick Campbell, had just launched her book on Trevor Howard in London. And now she was back to reap her crop. 'I'm afraid the picking is over,' she said. 'My *équipe* has been at it for the last three days. I wish you could have seen Madame Rotta winnowing the olives, tossing them up in the evening breeze. This spray of black olives flying through the air against the sunset was quite a picture.'

She added that she was taking her harvest to the mill that afternoon and asked if I would like to go with her. And so, within an hour, we were sitting in her dining room, tucking into a delicious lunch, before setting off for the mill of La Brague in Opio. As we finished our coffee, a young bearded giant arrived with his truck to transport Vivienne's olives to the mill.

To Gilbert, olive trees are sacred. And those who destroy them (he used the word assassinate) are no less than criminals. When he was digging foundations to build his house, he came across the great root of one of those murdered trees, deep down in the ground.

'Some of these roots', he said. 'weigh up to two tons each. I sliced a piece off it and stuck it in my garden. It is now a sturdy six-year-old, and it will be bearing fruit next year. But it won't be in full production for another twenty-five.'

By planting sections of these gigantic roots, you can, within a few years, have a new grove going back to Methuselah. On the other hand, if you take a cutting from a living, mature tree, it will grow into a fine fruit-bearing specimen, but it will only live three hundred years at most. Which presumably means that only the original stumps from the Garden of Eden have this immortal quality. Only fire or an intense frost will exterminate them. But, apart from these calamities, olive trees are indestructible as long as a morsel of the original roots remains in the ground.

Vivienne was lucky. When she bought her house thirty years ago, her trees were in perfect condition. 'The first thing I did was to have them pruned before I even touched the house,' she told me as we walked down to her car.

We led the way, with Gilbert and the olives, all 760 kilograms of them, following behind. When we arrived at the mill we came face to face with its gigantic waterwheel, still in use as late as 1972. Now the works have been updated with electrical equipment and centrifugal force.

The machinery was humming busily, working its way through the last load as we arrived. I watched it coming out at the end of its course – a thin yellow trickle, like camel's pee, obviously the produce of poor, anaemic trees. Vivienne, who had an appointment, was next on the list. Her nineteen sacks were emptied into a trough in the concrete floor. From there, moving slabs hoisted the olives up to a water-filled drum where all leaves, bugs and spiders were washed away. The fruit was then sucked up into the machinery, where it was crunched and mashed into a long, brown, oily snake. Out of it came a strange, warm smell. Afraid of missing the magic moment, I dashed to the end of the trough and watched the thick green oil plop heavily into a fifty-litre drum, the fruit of Vivienne's cherished, well-cared-for trees.

When it had all squelched through the electrical gut, and the last thick green drop had been squeezed out, the oil was weighed. Now the calculations began. Grabbing a scrap of paper, Vivienne scribbled her figures on it against the wall. The young man in charge did his sums with a bit of chalk on one of the great green vats reaching up to the ceiling.

'Sixty-four litres for Madame Glenavy,' he announced. 'Ça va, madame?'

'Oui, ça va.' And to me she added, 'The best part of it all is that our calculations match!' The grand total was 172 kilograms of oil, a liquid kilogram weighing more, in its own mysterious way, than a litre.

Madame Rotta, who had winnowed the olives in the sunset, stood by, watching unblinkingly. You could practically hear the sums clocking up in her head. She and her husband, who had done the picking, were getting two-thirds of the total. Originally from poverty-stricken Calabria, the Rottas had settled in Provence where they pursued, on very lucrative terms, the only trade they knew. And all the while, as the computer department of her brain ticked over, Madame Rotta rattled away incessantly, three words in local patois, ninety-seven in Calabrese. Although Vivienne nodded and smiled amiably, I could not help wondering how much she actually understood.

Once the weighing was done, we trooped off in a body to the office to pay the miller's fee. That also had to be divided, and this time Vivienne came off best, her share being one-third of the whole sum. As a registered grower, she will get a state reward in due course, a kind of subsidy based on the number of litres produced, as a contribution to encourage the maintenance of olive trees.

'This will take anything up to eighteen months to materialize,' she told me as we left.

The whole operation of producing 172 litres of first-class virgin olive oil had taken only two hours to complete.

'Are the stones crushed in the cylinder as well as the olives?' I asked the woman as we were leaving.

'Yes, everything is crushed together, then the pulp is dried off and used as fuel in the furnaces of the mill.'

'But what about the second and third pressings?' I asked. In some mills, they even used to do a fourth.

'Here,' she said firmly, 'we only do one. After the virgin oil has been squeezed out, the pulp is finished.'

As we left, cars were arriving thick and fast. Stumbling out of them came entire families bearing the fruit of their own two or three trees, in plastic bags and baskets. This kind of output all goes into the common pot. Only a master harvest like Vivienne's 780 kilograms warrants a pressing to itself.

As I had also missed the pruning session, I had to ask

Vivienne for a description of the process. 'They'll be pruning the olive groves at the mill tomorrow,' she told me. 'Why not come over and watch the operation?'

Young Thierry Occelli, the master pruner of the region, has one ruling passion – the cult of the olive. As this trend is now in decline there are fewer trees and fewer groves, so that by the late eighties there were 155 mills in action, compared with 825 in 1946.

Thierry and his men were already hard at work when we arrived at the grove of La Brague. In the tall, lush grass glistening around the trees were thousands of wild forget-me-nots, white rocket and scarlet poppies – red, white and blue, the colours of the French flag, all waving in the grass on that sparkling March afternoon.

Wading across the blooming grass, Thierry came over to meet us. 'Look at this,' he said, tapping at a gnarled, battered tree trunk. 'The frost got into it and the wood froze to death.'

The last three severe winters in the South of France have caused a great deal of damage in the olive groves. And there are other problems, which spread all over the tree in great cancer tumours.

'Do you believe in treatment?' asked Vivienne.

'As little as possible, and only for pickled olives. Nobody minds a few worms in the oil.' As for feeding, it simply doesn't come into the question. The soil of this valley, washed down from the surrounding heights since the beginning of time, is as rich as plum pudding.

Stroking a tree trunk beside him, he said, 'You would never guess, as you can't see them, but under this bark there are hundreds of "eyes", all fast asleep until pruning begins. At the touch of the knife they all wake up and spring into life, pumping up the sap with tremendous force. It is the life-blood of the new growth.'

We were now beside a thick mass of foliage quivering and shaking like a minor earthquake. 'This tree is just being started. There are two men inside it, and the youngest one is only sixteen, learning with my best chap, who did the same training as I did.'

A shower of leaves was raining out of the tree as its innards were being stripped from the centre. Light, air and sun being the most essential needs, its heart must be as bare as possible.

'How can they see the outline from inside?' I asked.

'Practice and experience,' came the answer.

'And you don't come down until the job is done?'

'Heaven forbid! It's inconceivable to cut from the ground . . .' And in conclusion he said, 'If ever you come across an olive tree at a crossroads, you can be sure a Roman soldier lies beneath it, complete with arms and shield. They were buried where they dropped in battle, and an olive was planted over them. There they still lie, undisturbed for the past two thousand years.'

The Romans, who also regarded the trees as sacred, used olive logs from pruning as boundary marks. Out of bounds was *extra oleas vagari*. Imbued with magic, the logs would keep the frontiers safe from enemies. The trees themselves were a symbol of peace, glory, wisdom and victory. The leaves were solely used for noble purposes, to decorate altars, temples and the heads of poets and generals. However, they only knew ten varieties of trees, out of the sixty that grow around the Mediterranean shores nowadays.

You don't 'grow' an olive tree. It is 'conducted' with all the respect and reverence due to a hero. And as part of the care and attention it demands, pruning is at the top of the list. The Romans, awed as they were by its nobility, dared only cut it back every eight years, whereas nowadays it is done every two or three years, which makes it infinitely more productive than in the past. But in spite of its increased value, farmers are still destroying their groves and selling the land for development, even though the law now forbids the destruction of trees without a special permit.

At the other end of the scale a new movement for promoting a more romantic approach to the whole business came into being in 1964, with the founding of a new order of chivalry, 'the Knights of the Olive Tree'. On election to the order, the members have to swear allegiance to the tree, 'to defend and protect it in word, deed and print, and to conduct themselves as faithful and honourable Chevaliers of the Brotherhood'.

Festivals known as Olivades take place every summer, attracting a vast number of tourists, resulting in much publicity for the cause, not to mention a handsome boost to the local economy. It is hoped, as a result, that existing trees will be more cherished and new ones planted and that olive oil in Provence will be restored to its traditional place of honour.

CHAPTER 8

The Holy Crusade

FOR some time I had been longing for a trip to the land of
the Cathars, where the Holy Crusade was launched against
them by the Pope and the King of France in 1209. I wanted
to explore their haunts and what was left of the mighty fortresses that had sheltered them in the last years of their lives.
So when Joanna rang up one morning to ask if I would join
her on a trip to Languedoc, I could hardly believe my ears.

'Let's start tomorrow morning,' she suggested.

Next day, after an early start, we headed west and made
for Tarascon, reaching it by lunchtime. There we found Good
King René's castle, which we had hoped to visit, closed until
June, and so we pushed on to Beaucaire, crossing the Rhône
by the only bridge I have ever heard of being blown away
by the wind – which happened here once on a boisterous
mistral day in 1875!

The magnificent thirteenth-century palace of Beaucaire, built
by the French king to celebrate his annexation of Provence
and Languedoc, had recently been restored to its original splendour
by the Beaux Arts Society. The rest of the town, as empty as
a church on a weekday, was being rebuilt street by street.
Most of these southern cities, poleaxed by the Inquisition, are
still in a state of shock and only just beginning to recover from
the battering they received seven hundred years ago.

The Cathar town of Minerve was totally deserted when we
reached it at midday. Without shops or markets, it had none
of the usual bustle common to southern towns. Peopled by
ghosts, it was still haunted by the visitation of the Holy Crusade in the thirteenth century. In the main square opposite
the church the Inquisitors had built a huge bonfire into which,

singing hymns, 180 Cathars of both sexes had walked of their own free will. A concrete slab now marks the spot. And opposite this modest monument stands the eleventh-century church firmly barred and bolted.

The Cathar phenomenon was only one of the many heresies of the Middle Ages, all of them searching for a way out of the murky spiritual darkness of the times. The general unrest and discontent were due in part to the start of the new millennium. The world had not come to an end as expected and nothing good had turned up instead. The Bible had been translated for the first time, and the difference between the original message of the Gospel and contemporary church teaching came as a shock to the faithful. Another reason for this epidemic of soul-searching was largely due to the debauched and decadent way of life of the clergy in Provence at the time. As a result, the neglected faithful had become disenchanted with their spiritual leaders. The Cathars' personal conduct and strict moral code stood in startling contrast to the unseemly behaviour of the local clerics and was a magnet to the people, who followed them in their thousands. Shining like a bright light in the superstitious gloom of the Middle Ages, they spread all over Europe at extraordinary speed. Giving away all personal property, they set off on a life of prayer and philanthropy. Known as the 'good men', they were so dedicated that out of 100,000 who were burnt at the stake only three recanted.

There was only one way for the Church to regain control of the masses, and that was by getting rid of the Cathars, who would have to be exterminated. Orders went out from Rome to the bishops of France to muster volunteers, and soon, with serfs and villeins in tow, great French lords and bishops came flocking to the banner and the Cross. By early June 1209, an enormous multitude 300,000 strong was assembled as a Holy Crusade under the leadership of Simon de Montfort.

The first town on the Crusade's visiting list was Béziers. There, 7000 citizens were massacred in the church, to be followed by the rest of the population. After it was over the leaders apologized to the Pope for killing only 25,000. They were in fact underselling themselves, as the grand total was found in the end to be over 60,000.

At Lavaur, resistance was organized by Dame Guiraude and eighty knights. She was raped and pushed down a well, with stones rolled in on top of her. The rest of the population walked into the enormous bonfire of their own free will.

At Bram, the castle, unequipped for a siege, fell in three days. The Governor was hanged. The garrison, over one thousand strong, had their noses sliced off and their eyes plucked out. Their leader, who had been left with one eye, was sent along the roads in charge of the sightless party, with all their eyes in a basket, to terrorize the neighbourhood.

As we reached the castle of Puivert, the rolling stock of a film unit in action surrounded the great walls. An attempt at scaling them was repulsed from above. Men on ladders were sent flying through the air, and boiling oil was apparently being hurled at the warriors below.

With half a dozen turrets in good order and a mighty dungeon surrounded by massive fortifications, the fortress has an irresistibly photogenic appeal for the film industry.

In its heyday Puivert was the summer residence of the aristocracy of Béziers. There, to amuse this discriminating nobility, all the troubadours of the South would gather for concerts, contests and competitions. Not only a centre of intellectual and artistic endeavour, the castle inmates also went in for sport and jousts and feats of arms, which succeeded one another to amuse the guests. It was a summer palace, a pleasure haunt, in no way made for war, siege or defence.

It was captured in three days.

There, the troubadours were the main prey. They had to be annihilated, so that the Occitan way of life could be wiped off the map once for all, with its independence, language and traditions, its subtle and sophisticated civilization, its amiable pastimes and all its elegant futility. With the destruction of Puivert society, a culture came to an end for ever.

At Termes it was water shortage that caused the downfall of the fortress. Although besieged by the Archdeacon of Paris and his famous war machines, it could have resisted indefinitely with an adequate water supply. After defeat, the castle was left standing, until it was levelled by Cardinal Richelieu in the seventeenth century. As an implacable enemy of medieval grandeur, and all nobility, one by one he demolished all the great fortresses, including Carcassonne, Beaucaire, Les Baux, Nice, Eze and countless others in his manic hatred of the power of medieval barons and the flamboyant chivalry for which they stood.

Lastours, a group of mighty castles built on top of a giddy perpendicular peak, was finally brought to heel through famine and water shortage. It would have been impossible for the massive pile to be captured by force. Built in the eleventh and twelfth centuries, these towers stood on chalky rock riddled with natural caves and tunnels. It is to this citadel that the people of Carcassonne are supposed to have fled, through underground passages, when their town was captured by the Pope's army.

It is no surprise to hear that the formidable stronghold of Peyrpertuse could not be overrun or captured by any means, either ruse or arms. In 1240, when Count Guillaume was besieged, the leader of the Crusaders offered to negotiate. The Count, who had been excommunicated, was pardoned in exchange for handing over his fortress. There was no bonfire on that occasion.

Even though the Crusaders had funked it, we were determined to have a go and make it to the top. And in spite of a gale hurling vicious needles of rain at the mountain, we attacked it with a will. Getting down on hands and knees, we squelched our way up the face of a cliff running with mud and water.

When we finally reached the fort, we found to our dismay that the entrance was on the opposite side. There was no other way but to creep round the enormous pile, hugging the walls that went down level with the precipice. Clinging to the ramparts with the wind lashing out in gusts, and hardly enough space for a toehold, we realized why this castle had never been captured. From the guidebook we had gathered that the climb was 'no spree for the faint-hearted' and that visitors were sometimes blown off the terraces by the wind. 'Terraces' was a euphemism for the great pile of rocks on the other side. Although the wind howled around the ruin, it felt more secure than the north face we had just scaled.

Built along the knife-edge crest of the peak, it is easy to see why it was never taken, and impossible to imagine how men, horses, war machines and supplies for the garrison could ever have reached such a spot. Perched up there among the clouds, winds and eagles, it must have been a joyless existence at the best of times. Above the tree-line as it is, there is no timber for winter fires. Very little game lives at these altitudes.

Finding food and keeping warm must have been a nightmare. Inaccessible to troubadours and their ilk, there was no entertainment of any kind. How did they survive the long, bleak winter evenings? The thought of life in those gloomy gothic castles on top of gale-swept peaks curdles the blood.

By the time we arrived at Puylaurens, on the Spanish border, the gale had gone up several notches on the 'force meter'.

Frozen and apprehensive, we stared at the Dantesque rock to which clung the ruin of the fortress. There is something a little eerie about these mountaintop strongholds. The mysteries of Rennes-le-Château, only a few miles away, hover almost palpably around these Cathar castles. The ink-black clouds, the howling gale, cawing rooks and general desolation of the place, made it all look like a Transylvanian backdrop to some Dracula Dreadful of the thirties.

After Aguilar, all the Cathar castles had surrendered by the middle of the thirteenth century. There was only Montségur left.

Snowdrifts lay by the roadside and freezing rain dripped out of the sky as we reached the field where 210 human beings were roasted alive for their faith seven hundred years ago. Way above our heads, floating like a grey ship in a bank of heaving mist, was the phantom stronghold of Montségur. Staring at it, almost 1300 metres up on top of the Pog, its perpendicular peak, my heart sank at the thought of the scramble ahead. This one seemed worse than all the others put together.

Puffing, groaning and cursing, we finally made it to the top. The entrance into one of the most famous medieval castles in the world is just a hole in the six-foot-thick wall of the fortress.

Inside, a few rough steps lead up to the battlements. From there the inner space seems so small that it is difficult to imagine over two hundred people living in it for several years. By the time I reached the top, Joanna was stamping around on the loose stones of the unprotected topmost level of the ramparts. Aiming her camera at the surrounding peaks, and down at the horrifying precipice below, she was clicking away in all directions as usual.

'Do look were you're putting your feet,' I implored her. Giddy with vertigo, I had to squeeze my eyes shut. By the time I had recovered enough for another look, the mist was rolling up the Pog like some huge tidal wave of ectoplasm. Coming level with the ramparts, it did a U-turn, crawled over the edge, then began to sink into the empty fortress. Crouching up there with the mist swirling all round, I could almost see and hear it all, the crackling of the fire, the smoke rising into the sky, the screams of the victims and the awful choking smell. Shivering at the thought I said, 'If we don't leave soon, we won't even be able to find our way down the mountain.'

CHAPTER 9

The Knights of the Temple

STILL engrossed in the Middle Ages, whenever I could get away from the garden chores, I was boning up on the tragic life story of the Knights of the Temple of Jerusalem. Up on the heights of La Gaude was one of their fortresses, which had been renovated throughout and was said to be completely restored to its original condition. Having admired it from afar I was longing to get into it and see the surroundings in which these remarkable men had lived. So I rang up the Syndicat d'Initiative in Vence to find out if it was open to visitors.

'Not that I know of,' said the girl at the end of the line. 'But you could always try. It belongs to the actress Vivienne Romance.'

As no phone number was available, I wrote her a note, in answer to which came a brief reply from her husband: a flat refusal. Madame Romance was too ill to see anyone at the moment, and anyway there was nothing more for her to tell than would appear shortly in her autobiography.

No other Templar castle has been so accurately restored as the fortress of La Gaude. The old Commanderie of St Martin above Vence, transformed into a luxury hotel, bears no resemblance to the original. As the master house of the area in the Middle Ages, it controlled the castles of Le Broc, St Laurent, Tourrettes and La Gaude. When it was restored in the twenties, the builders were said to have found the skeletons of a couple of girls in the foundations. The age-old belief that a castle with a virgin walled up alive in its battlements is impregnable crops up all over Europe. Who has not heard of a maiden castle?

In an effort to reduce constant warfare among the barons of the Middle Ages, the Popes had launched the Crusades to the Holy Land. This effectively put an end to their incessant private feuds. But what the Popes had not foreseen was the effect it would have on Provence. Reduced, impoverished and defenceless, the local nobility had no means left with which to fend off the endless Saracen raids and Spanish invasions that plagued its shores.

It was eventually the Knights of the Temple of Jerusalem who were to save the situation. This new order had sprung up in the Holy Land at the time of the First Crusade. The kind-hearted Hugo de Payen took it on himself to look after the bemused pilgrims who landed in Palestine in a state of shock. After months of trekking through Europe and sailing in filthy rat-infested ships, they arrived in a war zone with no fixed fighting line. You never knew who was your friend or your enemy. There was nowhere to stay or sleep. The food, when available, was bizarre, the water was undrinkable and sanitation non-existent. Those early religious tourists were bewildered by the climate, the crushing, sodden heat, the sandflies and the lice, the bandits and the beggars. As this was all too much for Hugo to cope with on his own, he enrolled his friend Geoffrey de St Omer, and several other knights who had been discarded by their lords, excommunicated by the Church or who were just bumming around. And so a kind of spiritual Foreign Legion for the protection of pilgrims in distress took shape.

In 1118 the Patriarch of Jerusalem, applauding their dedication, gave them land next to the Temple, from which they soon became known as the Knights of the Temple. Bearded and shaven-headed, the warrior-monks kept away from women, wine and meat and avoided all things pleasant, including personal hygiene. As bathing was discouraged, these high-minded men crawled with vermin and stank like drains. Before long there were 15,000 of them, with three times more minions, horse-grooms and men-at-arms. As a well-meaning but untidy, ramshackle and cumbersome force, they were encouraged by the Patriarch to go abroad as soon as possible. Taking the hint, Hugo de Payen set off for France in search of funds and to test the lie of the land.

Perhaps with an introduction from his patron in Jerusalem, he managed to get an audience with the Count of Provence, whom he instantly appointed Grand Master of the Knights of the Temple. From then on they became established as a police force to protect the province and fight off the endless raids and invasions of the Moors.

In 1139, by which time they had spread all over Europe, the Knights Templars came directly under the wing of the Vatican, which meant they were independent of kings and all other rulers. The Pope, who approved of their ideals, declared himself their overall protector, while total freedom in worldly and spiritual matters was left in their hands.

With such powerful backing combined with total independence, the Templars were soon a well-established and extremely competent international organization. And it was not long before they were acting as a bank to popes and kings, who regarded the Paris Temple as the most important money-market of Europe. These banker-warrior-monks invented the first cheque for the protection of travellers, as well as the 'mort-gage' system of finance.

Philippe le Bel, then King of France, and chronically short of cash, had already caused several riots by fiddling with state finances. As the Paris mob were out for his blood, he had taken refuge in the Temple, and it was then that he discovered the extent of its wealth. The solution to his problem as he saw it was, there and then, to confiscate the lot. But there was a snag. As the order was under Vatican protection, he could do nothing without the Pope's consent. Since this would have been out of the question, he immediately set up a public relations campaign to discredit the Templars in the eyes of the people. Accusing them of all sorts of imaginary crimes, such as sodomy, idolatry, dishonouring the Cross and so on, he ended up claiming that the Knights saw themselves as founders of a new Church to the Holy Spirit, in which the power of the Vatican would become obsolete. Since the Pope was the Knights' ultimate protector, the claim was untenable, without credibility. As he ignored the whole matter, the King realized there was only one thing he could do. And that was to found a new papacy of his own, which he did by establishing Bertrand de Goth as the first Pope of Avignon. From then on he was independent of Rome.

Claiming he was under orders from the Grand Inquisitor, Philippe had the Templars arrested on 13 October 1307. Im-

mediately rounded up throughout the entire kingdom, they
were interrogated under torture and burnt at the stake soon
after. Their enormous wealth was impounded by the Crown
and their castles handed over to the Knights of St John, later
to be known as the Knights of Malta.

As I scribbled away at the table in the garden, Desmond
telephoned.

'We are going up to the mountains to look at castles and
chapels,' he said. 'Would you like to come?'

'I'll be with you in half an hour,' I said.

Jumping into the Mini, I made for the Baou. At their house
we got into Desmond's car and set off at once.

The drive up the mountain to the tiny peak village of
Bézaudun was magic. As the summer always reaches the heights
later than the plain, the short grass was sprinkled with millions of early spring flowers. All round the horizon the saw-
edged peaks of the Alps formed a jagged, sugar-white rim,
glittering in the blinding sunlight.

Snaking along the crest of the Cheiron Range, our road
followed the path of Augustus on his way to crush the trucu-
lent tribes of Vence, two thousand years earlier.

With great excitement Desmond, who was on one of his
esoteric sprees, pointed out Mount Jerusalem, from which
he took a sighting to check his measurements. Every tiny
chapel lost in the wilderness, or perched on top of some
inaccessible rock, matched his grid system to the millimetre. Whenever we reached a new height he would say,
'Now, just down there on the other side, there should be a
chapel to mark the spot halfway between X and Y.' And
there always was. The fact that they were stamped with
the symbols of the Croix Patée, the triangle or the cosmic
sign of the swastika, did not surprise him in the least.
These always appeared wherever the Knights had lived.

According to Desmond, the numerous shrines stood as
markers in a huge survey established by the Temple, based
on the order's most important symbol, the triangle, represent-
ing the Trinity.

The distance from Mount Jerusalem to Bézaudun castle was
exactly 9000 metres. With the third angle of the triangle at
Puy-de-Tourrettes, also a precise 9000 metres away, the geo-
metrical figures matched to the millimetre.

In Desmond's notes on the area, I later read that the castle at Bézaudun fell short of the full 9000 by a few metres. Where the castle should have been was a junction of small mountain roads. At that exact spot stood a square-shaped, roughly hewn rock, with a Greek column topped by an elaborate nineteenth-century iron cross. The castle, which should have been built where this monument stood, was a few metres further south. Why wasn't it at the exact cross-section? we wondered. We were to find out the baneful reason for this only too soon.

Perched on a peak between two deep valleys, Bézaudun floats in the clouds, surrounded by a vast expanse of empty space, an ideal spot for a Templar castle. No one could ever approach unseen.

Desmond pointed to the strange monument at the cross-roads. 'The square rock at the base is certainly prehistoric,' he declared. 'I'm sure it was the Templars who planted the Greek column on top of it. Now I wonder why. Let's go and see what we can find out about it.' He stood aside to let me go first. Scrambling up on hands and knees, I grabbed the column to steady myself. On the right-hand side was a sheer drop of about seven metres down to the road below. Standing behind me, Desmond said, 'Give it a tap to see what it sounds like.' I did.

'Well,' he said, 'that sounds pretty funny. Try lower down.' The pillar, which sounded hollow, gave out a deeper tone. I went on tapping at various points, and every time a different sound rang out.

The wind had suddenly come up and was now howling round us in a menacing way. 'I think that's enough,' said Desmond. 'Let's get down or we'll be blown off our perch.'

We set off to explore the village. On the doors of the twelfth-century church built against the castle walls a large swastika was carved on the wooden panel. The other two symbols appeared here and there as well, throughout the village.

By then the sun was beginning to dip behind the western Alps, and it was growing cold. Setting off down the mountain, we made for home. I was feeling strangely whacked, light-headed and faintly queasy. By the time I got home, I was shivering so much that I had to go to bed. Next day I felt worse. When I rang up Desmond next day, he said he was feeling pretty ropy, but not as bad as last night.

As the days went by, I felt less and less well. It was an

enormous effort to get up in the mornng. The walls spun round, and sometimes I had trouble in finding the floor.

Four weeks later I was in King Edward VII Hospital in London for extensive medical tests. All results were negative. There was nothing the matter with me. The specialists were mystified. In the end it was a doctor in Monte Carlo who got me back on my feet, with powerful tonics and massive doses of vitamins. He said I was so depleted he was surprised I could still manage to stagger around. After a year my hair stopped dropping out and my nails no longer came off in layers. I could see clearly, without double vision. My hands stopped shaking, and I could sleep up to five hours a night.

Desmond thought he knew the cause of my malaise. Without realizing it at the time, we had hit a high energy point at the crossroads in Bézaudun. The Templars, who knew of its disintegrating powers, had built their castle out of reach of the danger spot. As a warning, they marked the place with the Greek column. In the nineteenth century the Church came along and added the cross. If he was right, I had caught the full blast of the destructive energy. By tapping it all over, I had stirred up its powers and suffered the consequences.

Desmond's firm belief is that the Templars were researching into natural laws and phenomena, something that would have been condemned as witchcraft if they had carried out their experiments in the open. But working in secret must have made them appear even more suspect. As it was, their general competence and independence of mind was a real menace to the King. All the best brains not recruited by the Church flocked to the Order of the Temple. There were therefore far too many brilliant men among them, a potential danger that had to be eliminated.

So once more the coast of Provence was left unprotected against the constant invasions that were to continue unmolested for several centuries to come.

CHAPTER 10

The King That Never Was

Annexed by France, the land of Occitania had gone. *La langue d'Oc*, the language of the troubadours, was systematically eradicated, with French enforced everywhere as the official idiom. Now came the turn of Provence proper. The last act of its independent existence was to be played out in a fantastic and flamboyant manner. Ironically this was brought about by the weakness and lassitude of the most gifted and popular ruler who had ever reigned in the South.

Of all people, Good 'King' René, Duke of Anjou, Count of Provence and King of Naples and the Two Sicilies, was born in 1409 at the period in history most timely for his temperament, his tastes and his talents – if not for the fortunes of Provence.

Often described as the first of the Humanists, he fervently followed the trail laid by the troubadours. His reign coincided with the end of an era based on spiritual values, honour and courtesy that entirely suited his own character. Optimistic, open-minded and trusting, René was as much a gentleman as a great nobleman. Hating anything underhand, treacherous or disloyal, there was nothing tawdry or calculating in his make-up. With his romantic nature, he lived in a world of high adventure, medieval chivalry and flamboyant feats of arms. In spite of being continually let down and betrayed, he lost neither his equanimity nor his serene belief in justice and basic human decency. Taking bad luck in his stride, he never bore anyone a grudge. His unshakeable good nature was disarming.

The death of his father when René was only eight, gave his mother, Yolanda of Aragon, the chance to become Regent of Anjou. Taking the young Dauphin away from the King and

Queen of France (an unreliable pair), she brought him up with her own children. In this way the ambitious Yolanda was able in due course to marry her own daughter to the heir of the French throne, thus making him her son-in-law.

In 1424, when René was fifteen, she betrothed him to Isabelle, daughter of the Duke of Burgundy. Having no brother, Isabelle became Duchess of Bar and Lorraine on her marriage, and René, as her husband, took over the two provinces as their Duke. All this scheming would have worked to perfection if Burgundy had not backed England against the French Crown at the time. As it was, poor fifteen-year-old René was trapped between an overbearing, tyrannical mother, fanatically religious and pro-French, and a father-in-law who helped the English army against France and Joan of Arc. But with his usual optimism and serene disposition, René sailed through the impossible situation with unimpaired morale and soaring popularity.

Soon after his wedding he was attacked by the Duke of Burgundy's nephew, who claimed Bar and Lorraine for himself. And so off to war the teenage youth had to go, to defend his wife's inheritance and his own share in it.

After three years of hard fighting, René finally won the day. A well-earned victory but the only one in a long life of constant wars and skirmishes, all of which he heartily detested. Much more to his taste was the cultured court of Lorraine, where painters, poets and musicians were always welcome. All through his life he was to encourage the 'New Art', just beginning to arrive from Renaissance Florence. As well as the last great feudal ruler, he was also the most influential art patron of the period. At his court in Anjou, he encouraged poetry, music, the theatre, architecture, garden design, pageantry, horse trials and hunting. He loved flowers, fine clothes, panache, books, women, clowns, dwarfs, exotic birds, troubadours and all kinds of outlandish creatures.

Surrounded by his minstrels, monks, 'Moors' in costume, jugglers and acrobats René was blissfully happy. His greatest pleasure lay in perambulating his motley crew through the streets and showering presents all round. This way of life demanded the sort of fortune he never had. His wild generosity was described, not surprisingly, as extravagance by his enemies. But the people of Provence, who enjoyed it all as much as he did, were always prepared to pay more taxes to keep the circus going. As good Southerners, they loved display,

flamboyance, drama, anything unusual, exaggerated or spectacular. Through these perennial processions, festivals, reviv-
als of early medieval plays, street musicians and public dancing,
René earned life-long popularity.

All these expenses, which were enormous, were recorded
down to the last ducat and the accounts stuffed into canvas
bags hooked to the ceiling of the counting house at the Court
of Anjou. In this way they were saved from the voracity of rats
and are still available as proof of Good King René's goings-on.

Never left in peace for very long, a new war was soon
waged against him by the successor to the last Duke of Burgundy, with the help of his English and Flemish allies. Defeated and taken prisoner, René spent a whole year locked
up in the dungeon of Isabelle's cousin. But the Duke's library
was available to him, and to pass the time he studied Greek,
Latin and Hebrew, mathematics, astronomy and architecture.
Released for a few months, he was recaptured for another
two-year stretch, during which time he took up music and
landscape gardening, wrote poetry and calmly started to paint
a portrait of his gaoler, the great bully who took so much
pleasure in tormenting him. It was while thus engaged that
René became Count of Provence and King of Naples and the
Two Sicilies.

Isabelle, who governed her duchy with great skill and wisdom, decided to claim the throne of Naples on his behalf. It
was thought a good thing to keep French influence alive on
the spot in Italy; although of course, at the same time, English
influence on French territory was considered treacherous and
intolerable. But that is another story.

Acclaimed with wild enthusiasm by the population of Naples,
Isabelle was soon harassed by King Alfonso of Aragon, who
was entrenched in the seashore castles of Ovo and Nuovo a
little further down the coast. Having already snatched Sicily
away from the French, he was now determined to take Naples
over as well.

Without funds or troops of any kind, Isabelle was losing
ground fast. In desperation she appealed to Burgundy to release her husband. This was agreed in exchange for several
castles and one million pieces of gold, to be collected from
his loyal subjects of Bar, Lorraine, Anjou and Provence. Free
at last, René set off for his Angevin court, where he spent the
next two years in romantic dalliance. With all his interests

and activities, how he found time for his innumerable mistresses and his multitude of bastards is a mystery. But of course his real vocation, he always claimed, was quite different, and he would have been a monk if he had had the choice.

Finally submitting to his wife's desperate pleas for help, he arrived in Naples early in the summer of 1438, to be greeted with lavish festivities by the delirious population. But it was much too late. After three weeks of these giddy goings-on he found himself surrounded by Alfonso's army.

When it came to pitched battle, René's methods were more spectacular than effective. Waving his double-edged sword over his head, he would charge on his warhorse, shouting his battle-cry of 'Anjou-Provence' without looking back to see if his knights were following behind.

The last hand of the battle was played by the enemy with the well-known trick of crawling through subterranean drains and tunnels and suddenly springing out of the ground everywhere at the same time.

René just managed to escape with his life and a handful of followers.

Arriving in Provence after the débâcle in Naples, he found his brother-in-law, now King of France, holding court in Toulouse. Huge celebrations were instantly planned, as if a great victory was being celebrated. No defeat or disaster could ever get René down. From then on, having lost his Italian kingdom, he wandered from one castle to another, followed along the roads by enormous processions of burghers and peasants, ecstatic at having him back at last from his futile foreign wars.

Reviving an old legend of the local river dragon, Tarasque of Tarascon, René founded a new order of chivalry, the Knights of the Tarasque. A huge model of the monster, six metres long and twice a man's height, was constructed, and paraded once a year through the streets, propelled and driven by sixteen men walking inside the great hulk, shooting fireworks through its nostrils and braying like growling thunder. Meanwhile the huge tail thrashed to right and left, crashing into people along the way. A really successful day demanded several accidents with cracked skulls and broken limbs. When the yearly procession takes place nowadays, the Tarasque travels more sedately on well-oiled wheels, driven by half a dozen men, its tail firmly screwed on, no longer lashing out and demanding victims.

King René's next great project was setting up a model farm at Gardane, near Aix. As master and farm hands were to enjoy the same comfort, the royal castle and the peasants' cottages were to be equally up to date in every way. There was to be one standard for both the King and his people. The most modern agricultural techniques were applied. Only prize cattle and sheep were bought and bred.

In December 1457, René arrived in state for the official opening of the farm, followed as usual by a procession of local inhabitants, monks, musicians and jugglers, with flocks of aristocratic sheep and the noble heads of protesting cattle bringing up the rear. A great feast was held in the grounds, and dancing went on all night.

The regular fixtures of the agricultural year were like staged performances. Shearing took place in public, after which the flocks, led by shepherds in white robes decorated with the royal arms, set off for the summer pastures. On their way back in the autumn, they were greeted by the King's musicians and led back to the farm, escorted by the entire court. The camel corps, led by a 'little Moor' in gold and scarlet velvet, headed the cortège. Then followed the menagerie, complete with monkeys astride gazelles and parrots riding ostriches. After them came the courtiers, local peasants, beggars, cripples and highwaymen. Nobody was ever left out of these glorious homecomings. But times have changed. No shepherd is greeted quite like that on his return from the high pastures nowadays.

After a long, busy, enjoyable life, the ageing monarch was growing weary. More and more of his time was spent on the farm and, although he still organized great bear and wolf hunts, he no longer took part in them.

The new King of France, Louis XI, who had succeeded René's brother-in-law, was feared and hated by all his subjects. Dishonest and a notorious liar, he was obsessed with grabbing lands and castles wherever he could. Hearing that René had left him nothing in his will, he immediately attacked him on grounds of high treason. Feeling too old and spent to fight, René decided for the sake of peace, to let him have Anjou. Deliriously happy, the people of Provence realized they would now have their King with them for good. Encouraged by their enthusiasm, he resumed his tours with the court, stopping on the way here and there to give free shows of his jugglers and dancers, always followed by a roadside barbecue.

Forever spending and giving away money he had not got, René realized that funds had to be raised somehow, so he began to borrow from Italian lenders. Jews came to the rescue as well, in exchange for which many measures against them were suppressed. And so, with the coffers replenished, the festivals and processions, the jugglers and the acrobats were off on their merry rounds again.

But all this rejoicing came to a sudden end when René died in 1480, aged seventy-one, and the King of France annexed Provence.

This act of 'treachery' rankles in the minds of Southerners to this day. Fiercely independent as they are, they have never got used to the idea of losing their freedom. No doubt their ferocity during the French Revolution was due to pent-up rage and resentment over the generations, which found its release in the horrors of the guillotine at Grasse and Marseilles.

This is the last of Provence as an independent state. The following centuries, up to the present time, belong to the history of France and have nothing to do with this tale.

CHAPTER 11

Fireworks and Races

MEANWHILE at Mas Mistral the nightingales, who had been at it since the beginning of May and were still going strong, had another ten exhausting days to go. It was a constant, non-stop twenty-four hours on duty, and the chorus would continue until the last day of the month. On the morning they sang their final notes, we drove over to Monaco for the great event, the annual race – the Grand Prix of Monte Carlo.

During the entire month of May, the Principality had been gradually transformed. Huge stands had gone up all over the town. The Casino Gardens were hedged in with stout wire fences straight out of Colditz, while the palm trees were encased in armour-plated corsets. Steel barriers lined the streets and every lamp-post was decorated with megaphones. Great bales of straw had been dumped along the pavements, and television trucks were entangled in miles of wiring. Policemen, more numerous than ever, padded up and down the boulevards, diverting traffic into dark forgotten streets left over from the last century. There were first-aid posts and ambulances at every hairpin bend. Through loudspeakers nestling in orange trees along the avenues sprightly tunes and rock and roll music boomed out all over the town. For four glorious days the deafening roar of racing cars tearing and screeching through the streets drowns every other sound. All shops are closed. There is a general holiday spirit, visitors from overseas wear funny hats and everybody has a wonderful time. Since Monte Carlo is minute (the whole Principality could fit into Central Park, with room to spare) the course has to run through the town. The race takes place in Ascension week at the end of May, with the trials on Thursday and Friday and the race itself at the weekend.

As we had received an official invitation, we watched the race from the top terrace of the Hôtel de Paris, instead of the balcony of our new flat round the corner. Leaning over the balustrade, our champagne glasses wobbling on the ledge, we peered down at the cars screeching round the murderous V-bends and along Boulevard Albert 1er down by the harbour. The noise coming up from below was deafening. Several people whose eardrums were splitting went inside to watch it all on television. Patricia, the English wife of Prince Rainier's Chancellor, came over to join us.

'The noise is quite awful,' I said. 'Shall we go inside?'

'No,' she answered firmly. 'I like my thrills live and raw.'

As we felt the same way ourselves, we stayed on the terrace till the end of the race.

Heavy, low-slung cars, some like monstrous science-fiction insects, others with wide, splayed-out wheels and covered with advertisements for cigarettes, tyres, headlights and so on, hugged the road like squashed turtles.

Everything was going well until suddenly a sound like a clap of thunder came up from below. A couple of cars had crashed into each other, just beneath our terrace. There was a horrific grinding screech and smoke billowed out of the crumpled vehicles. Appearing instantly, a breakdown truck disentangled the mangled carcasses. The pilots staggered to the side, and the race started up again immediately.

As we stood on the terrace, champagne corks went on popping all round until sunset. The guests, most of the international set in residence at the time, were in high good humour. All over the Principality, and in the millionaires' yachts in the harbour below, the same rejoicings were taking place. As a warm evening breeze floated in from the sea, everybody toasted the event of the year.

On our return I decided to tackle my old friend Raymond Broad, ex-Riviera correspondent of the London *Evening News*, on the history of the Grand Prix. Sitting at a table of the Régence in Vence, a bottle of wine between us, I grilled him on the subject. There was nothing he did not know about it. Over the years he had covered more races than he could remember.

The Grand Prix originally emerged from the Monte Carlo Rally, which takes place in the second fortnight of January.

For four days and nights the cars race through the *départements* of Drôme, Isère, Ardèche and the Alps of Haute Provence. Their crazy, fanatical fans spend the entire time encamped day and night in snow and ice on the most dangerous bends of the route, where the cars come screeching round in howling mountain gales. These quirky rally drivers thrive on the appalling weather conditions and thoroughly enjoy the horror of the whole performance.

'It all goes back to the first race which was won by the Frenchman Rougier. At that time the most popular cars were Hotchkiss, Renaults, Fords and Delahayes. Only the best cars of the time are ever used,' Raymond said.

In those early days the roads of Europe were still embedded in the Middle Ages. There were no services or rescue teams of any kind.

'If you came across an avalanche in your path,' Raymond went on, 'or tumbled into a ditch, you had to dig yourself out with your gardening tools. That's where the Rally's emblem of a pick and shovel came from. In those days the thing was done for a lark. Here and there, all round Europe, people would stuff their cars with crates of champagne and set off for "dear old Monte". When they arrived they joined their friends who had done the same thing. And while the champagne was cooling in the ice boxes of the Hôtel de Paris, they spent many a happy hour polishing up their cars for the Concours d'Elégance next day. Nowadays, of course, the filthier their cars are, the more prestige and acclaim they get. A "concours de mud".

'On one occasion, a man who had entered the Rally with his wife found himself with a problem on his hands. The co-pilot's minimum weight is sixty-five kilos. And she only tipped forty-five. "Don't you worry," said this ingenious fellow to his skinny wife as he hopped out to pick up a sack lying by the roadside. "This must weigh at least twenty kilos. It will bring us up to scratch." And off they set with the sack on board, never noticing the fine green powder oozing through the loose weave of the jute bag.'

'Having driven through the night, the pair arrived in Monte Carlo dyed a bright lettuce green from top to toe. And the more they scrubbed, the deeper it sank into the skin. As it turned out to be a bag of copper sulphate for spraying vines, they spent the next few days parading their brilliant green complexions before the astonished crowds of Monte Carlo.'

In 1951, Raymond went on, the Rally changed from this cosy amateur status to a highly organized competitive event with heavy commercial sponsorship.

'How could such a thing have happened?' I asked.

'When you change your tyres eighty to a hundred times during the race, it tends to become expensive, so they agreed to whatever advertising their backers insisted on.'

'When did the Grand Prix evolve from the Rally?' I asked.

'Way back in 1924, the Automobile Club of Nice made a terrible hash of a trial they were organizing for Monte Carlo. Several cars were damaged, and their drivers ended up in hospital.'

'Why didn't Monte Carlo look after its own affairs?' I asked.

And, as Raymond told me, that is exactly what happened. Monte Carlo joined the International Sport Commission, and from then on they looked after themselves from start to finish.

I was also much intrigued by those extraordinary racing cars. Why did they have to look so outlandish? It seems to be a question of gripping as much road surface as possible.

'They have to go as fast as they can,' said Raymond.

'Aren't they all the same? How can any one go faster than the others?'

'You *can* do something to help yourself. The car itself can't be tampered with, but there's nothing against polishing up its innards.'

'You mean the engine?'

'Exactly. It will literally go twice as fast once you've got it all shining like a mirror.' My mind boggled as he went on. 'The cylinder is a cast job, quite roughly machined, on account of the cost. But if you take it out and rub it thoroughly with grinding powder, your car will go like a bird.'

'So if they all do this, how can anyone win?' I asked, still puzzled.

'The skill of the driver. You get people like Makinen the Finn, the most amazing driver who ever lived, who could run his car twice as fast as any one else without ever losing his grip. He roared along at a hundred miles an hour. He had wonderful hands and a ballet dancer's touch on the pedals. He knew the precise moment to break, to de-clutch and when to give it a little throttle, when the ordinary driver would be screaming in his seat and standing on the brake. But Makinen had his throttle open. The combination of the throttle open and the brake on sounds crazy, but it's not, you see,' Raymond concluded.

And now, I could hardly wait for next year's race, which I would certainly be watching with a great deal more attention to the rules and subtleties of the game.

The next great excitement in the Principality is the fireworks competition, in which any country in the world can take part. Most of the international crowd hold dinner parties on fireworks nights. And the entire population of Monaco stands on its balconies facing the harbour, from which the rockets are launched.

The first display of that year happened to be a British production. And to everybody's surprise it turned out to be the most magnificent spectacle for a very long time. The press were lyrical in their praise and for once quite forgot their usual sarcastic remarks and sly digs at anything Anglo-Saxon. The report of the show in *Nice-Matin* next day claimed that the British performance had outshone all the efforts of other countries, including Italy and China, over the last few years. We felt modestly gratified.

Clutching our glasses, we stood on the balcony of the new flat with our assembled guests. As usual all the boats, from small craft to giant yachts, had steamed out of harbour before dark and now stood at anchor in the bay, bobbing up and down on the gentle swell and glowing like clouds of fireflies. Above them a bright orange moon was putting on a spectacular show of its own, duly reflected in the water around the boats. From where we stood, just above the port, it looked as if it had all been staged for our own personal benefit.

Shooting and swishing up to our level, the rockets exploded, the huge 'flowers' burst, blossomed and stood still in mid-air, frozen in space, level with our balcony. As they dissolved and glimmered away, new sprays flared up, swelled, multiplied and finally fizzled out. The shock waves of the explosions were so violent that I had to use a tin tray as a shield to save my ribs from being blown apart. I noticed that the rest of the company had withdrawn into the room, away from the repeated battering of the blast.

When it was over, the boats steamed back into harbour with foghorns hooting the most enthusiastic tribute we had ever heard. The entire population of the Principality, hanging over its terraces and balconies, clapped, yelled and cheered non-stop for the next twenty minutes. As far as we could remember, no fireworks display had ever had such a spectacular, thundering reception.

CHAPTER 12

Monaco on the Sea

THERE is a long tradition in which the reigning princes have encouraged the arts in Monaco. Prince Honoré would go all the way to Versailles to spend an evening at the theatre with his friend the King of France. Prince Louis I was an opera enthusiast, and Prince Antoine enjoyed conducting the palace orchestra. So it was in keeping with family tradition for Prince Charles to include a theatre for drama and opera as part of the casino complex. And for this he commissioned the architect Charles Garnier, who had built the Paris opera house.

But there is another aspect of Monaco's activities which is known to very few people – and that is the enormous amount of scientific work carried out in the Principality. As I knew how very much involved Monaco is with the oceans of the world, I asked the Director of the International Hydrographic Organization if he could fill me in on what this involves.

'Has it always been based here?' I asked as I sat opposite him in his office.

'The idea was dreamed up at a conference in Washington in 1899. Finally twenty-four nations agreed to meet in London in 1919. It was then decided that the oceans were too vast to be tackled and surveyed by each country on its own. It seemed more sensible to join forces and co-ordinate their activities. It was then that the IHO was founded as an idea. To become operative it needed a base which was fairly central, accessible, neutral and beside the sea. At this point Prince Albert, passionately interested in all the secrets of the oceans of the planet as he was, offered the Commission a free base in Monaco. In exchange he was to be kept informed, on an international scale, of all its findings.

'So we came in 1920, and have been in Monaco ever since, rent-free, on very generous conditions,' said the Director.

'There are now fifty-seven major member states around the world, all producing sea charts. This covers everything to do with the sea, not only shipping safety, but also fishing, yacht harbours and marinas and, of prime importance, offshore boundaries out at sea. The excellent rapport and co-operation between all those countries is based on the necessity to share information on a worldwide basis. Each member produces a chart of the area of interest to that country. Three of them, the United Kingdom, the United States and Russia bring out documents covering the whole world. Most European nations survey their own shorelines and any other parts of interest to them. Each one sends a copy of all they publish to us here in Monaco. We have a unique collection of 21,000 charts for all those countries, every one of which has been inspected by us for quality.'

It is essential for every mariner at sea to have a chart. There is now a new agreement stipulating that when a big ship enters a port it must be inspected by the local marine department of the country involved. If the captain has not got the necessary documents, he may be held until he can obtain them, so as to prove that he is capable of navigating a ship.

Back in my flat, as I sorted out my notes, an announcement came over Radio Monte Carlo about a foreign launch that had sliced its way through a yacht in the Mediterranean, cutting it neatly into two halves. Obviously the captain of this launch had not done his homework and did not know the laws of the sea.

Next on my list came the Museum, which forms part of the Centre Scientifique de Monaco, which also includes the International Laboratory of Marine Radio Activity. The aims of the Centre Scientifique are threefold: to continue studying all sea matters in their aspects; to apply all discoveries to the benefit of mankind; and to co-operate with international research.

Not quite knowing where to start, and not for the first time, I approached the Palace Chancellor for advice.

'Go and see the Commandant who runs the Museum. Nobody knows more about it than he does. I will speak to him.'

So one morning I found myself in the Commandant's light airy office perched high above the sea, which gleamed almost white under the ferocious noonday sun.

'Can you tell me about the aims and the achievements of the Museum?' I asked.

'Well,' he said, taking a deep breath, 'it all started with Prince Albert who was fascinated by the sea. For thirty years of his life he cruised up and down the oceans of the world in his various yachts.

'Entirely dedicated to scientific research, the Prince built the Museum as a Temple to Science. Opened in 1910, this was meant as a working laboratory for the Centre Scientifique, which he had founded in Paris four years earlier. Then, in 1960, the Museum, under the guidance of its President, Captain Jacques-Yves Cousteau, was remodelled and enlarged, so that it now occupies eight floors of the building. Together with the Faculté des Sciences in Nice, they study marine biology, the geological formation of the coast and the chemistry of the sea.

'When at the time of the Chernobil disaster nuclear particles floated over to our shore, the Director gave a lecture on the subject to reassure the public.

'Keeping an eye in all directions, this department also watches the weather. And, more crucial still, as Monaco lies in a sensitive area, special computers register earth tremors at all times of the day and night. Dating by radio carbon, which started as a sideline, has developed to such an extent that the Centre Scientifique now works on an international basis.'

I then inquired about the two mini submarines at the Museum's entrance. One, I was told, is a one-man model for short dives and the second, a two-seater, can stay twenty-four hours under water. In the main hall itself is a much larger diving saucer, kept for exploring deep Atlantic waters.

'How do you train your divers? Is there a special school for that?' I asked.

'No,' said the Commandant. 'Diving is like riding a bicycle. All our divers do other jobs as well. They have to feed the fish in underwater cages, collect deep-sea specimens, repair water cables and so on. Two years ago, they found a collection of Greek vases off the Marquet Beach in Fontvieille.'

A couple of scientific boats, the *Ramoge* and the *Winneretta-Singer*, cruise around, constantly checking the water. The *Ramoge*, which stands for St Raphaël, Monaco and Genoa, is financed by France, Monaco and Italy, with all decisions having to be enforced by the three states. The *Winneretta*, presented to the Museum by the Singer-Polignac Foundation, cruises along the African coast, studying geological formations and collecting deep-sea fish for the aquarium. It also studies the evolution of continents, which seem to be permanently on the move. The North Atlantic is now a hundred feet wider than in the days of Columbus, and the Pacific is stretching even faster.

It was Prince Rainier's idea to set up a commission with France and Italy to control the coastal waters of the Ligurian Sea. This operation is doing a valiant job with the help of another three scientifically equipped boats, constantly testing the state of the surrounding sea. *Nice-Matin* of 21 and 22 July 1987 reported that the coral and sea anemone reserve between Eze and Monaco was in decline, undermined by pollution, whereas the fish park of Larvotto, which comes right up to the shore, shows no signs of damage. This little paradise created by the Prince in 1975 literally sparkles with all kinds and manner of fish life. Here you can throw crumbs to large, healthy and tame fish, which frolic around as you wade among them. And other parts of the Monte Carlo coastline are so clear that you can actually count the minute crabs grazing in the fields of seaweed on the bottom.

The vast central hall on the ground floor of the Museum displays some of the submarines used by Captain Cousteau, and a quaint two-seater rocket for zooming around among the fish. Also on the ground floor is a collection of models of fishing boats and a variety of objects made out of sharks' backbones, as well as lumps of amber stuffed with insects. Ambergris is ambre gris, a fatty substance coughed up by sperm whales. It is unbelievably expensive, as it fulfils some obscure function in the making of scent. If you were lucky enough to find one of these greasy lumps washed up on the beach, it would make your fortune.

And now for some of the games which the sea plays with the sun. To begin with its red rays disappear in water at a depth of sixty to one hundred metres. Greens vanish below that. Three hundred and fifty metres further down, only brilliant dark blue is left. In very clear water, violet rays can reach another 350 metres deeper. After that is perpetual night.

Another surprising discovery I made was that the 'silent

sea' is an exploded myth. The uproar below the surface is quite as deafening to the denizens of the deep as our daily traffic noise is to us. But, on the whole, life for the populations of the sea is much easier to handle than for those on land. The most fragile forms can float like feathers without the slightest effort. Think of an armada of Portuguese man-of-war jellyfish cruising effortlessly on the high seas and then stranded in the noonday sun on a hot beach. Most sea creatures, largely filled with water, weigh much the same as their environment. With the flick of its tail a fish can shoot forward at lightning speed. How far does a dog get by wagging its stump?

Some of the fish in the aquarium, on the lower ground floor, have names like butterflies. The Red Emperor is a handsome creature with wide scarlet stripes. Sea cows with horns on their heads hobnob with boxfish, who are much the same shape and size. Among the more spectacular beauties are the purple surgeon fish, tiger fish and the yellow wrasse with its long thin beak furnished with a minute hole at the end. A puffer with a sloping forehead and a bemused expression on its face has complicated portholes, out of which the fins, flapping like wings, emerge. Blue devils, peacock puffers and all kinds of clown, hawk, comet and angel fish waltz around in perfect harmony. As I stood transfixed in front of a large tank in which half a dozen scorpion fish were putting on a stunning show, all their fins and wings and feathers floating slowly around them in a leisurely kind of aquatic ballet, a voice behind me suddenly said, 'Those make very good soup. What a waste!'

CHAPTER 13

Midsummer Night

BACK at Mas Mistral, it was lunch time. Pierre stood at the barbecue, roasting his famous duck soaked in brandy. With its delicate flavour too subtle to pinpoint, it was succulent. Pierre was an inspired cook. So there we were, sitting around the table, enjoying our lunch with the help of several bottles of Côtes du Rhône. Apart from the racket of the cicadas in the pine trees, the hour was calm and still.

Just then, disturbing our noontime peace, the pop-pop of a small Vespa was heard labouring up the hill. Within seconds it bounced into sight. His ample form bulging on either side of the tiny machine, a portly country policeman chugged towards us. Somewhat apprehensively I went over to greet him.

'Good morning, Monsieur l'Agent,' I said, wondering what nasty surprise he had in store for us. The last time we had a visit from one of his colleagues, he was firing across the garden at a fast retreating figure racing through the trees. When I opened the door the gun was aimed at my head. 'You are hiding him. Where is he? Hand him over or I'll shoot,' shouted the Law. And it took me quite a while to convince him that the man he was after had vanished through the garden. But this time our visitor was in a jovial mood and his revolver was in its holster, sticking out from his rotund behind, a reassuring sign.

'Bonjour, bonjour,' he panted affably.

'Have you come to arrest us?' I asked.

'Not this time. I saw you from the top of the hill, all sitting out here in the shade, and as I've got to write my report before I get back to the station I thought I would come and do it here with you. If you don't mind, that is.'

'Delighted,' said Anne. 'Have a glass of wine.'

'Ah, bien volontiers!' And the plump arm of the law settled down, spreading out his papers among the dishes on the table. One glass went down in a flash, sucked up noisily through the grey bristles of his moustache. Soon he was into the duck as well. 'Ah, this is life,' he sighed voluptuously as Anne refilled his glass.

'What is your report about?' she asked.

'The man who keeps raping old dames in the district. You haven't had any trouble with him yourselves, I hope.'

'No,' we both replied rather stiffly. Although middle-aged, we didn't think of ourselves as old dames.

'Well, don't go out alone at night, that's my advice,' wheezed our man, knocking back another glass of wine.

'I thought he had been caught?' said Anne. 'We heard you had arrested someone and that he was behind bars.'

'Correct, but that's the wrong man. That one is innocent.'

'Then why don't you let him go,' I asked.

'We won't be able to keep him much longer. His lawyer is raising hell. That's the trouble. We have now got to find the real villain. That's my orders.'

'And what if you can't catch him? What then?'

'That's only too likely, I'm afraid. But at least with one man inside, it won't look as if we've done nothing at all about it,' he said, gathering up his papers. 'And now I must go and hand in my report. Thanks a lot for the wine. And, you ladies, come and see me if you have any trouble.' With that he eased his hindquarters on to the tiny saddle and off he went, free-wheeling down the hill.

The minute he was gone we started to clear away the wreckage. There was a lot of work to be done before dinner. That evening we were celebrating two events. Pierre's return from Paris, for one thing. There he had at last found a doctor who pronounced his heart fit to fly. For many months past he had been turned down by innumerable medics who refused him the clearance he needed to carry on with his flying lessons. But now that he had it at last, we were rejoicing with him.

It was also Alan's birthday. As their only son, he was much spoiled by his parents. In Nice, he shared a flat with his girlfriend Nad, and they were both on holiday from Nice University. Nad was filling in time doing a holiday job at the Syndicat d'Initiative in Vence.

As it was Midsummer's Eve, we were also, willy-nilly, celebrating the feast of St John, as the event is known in these
parts. As protector of the crops in the fields, John is by far
the most popular saint in Provence.

In spite of the efforts of Mother Church to take over and
christianize all pagan practices that couldn't be stamped out,
it had not been easy to absorb the summer solstice celebrations. There is still a good deal around the edges that has
escaped conversion. In days gone by spontaneous village festivities often turned into riotous affairs. But in a prosperous,
up-and-coming community like Vence all feasts of this kind
are now as much as possible under the control of the Folklore Committee. Having been to some of their meetings, I
know just how rigid and inflexible they can be. Only fluent
Provençal linguists are admitted. Their costumes must be of
genuine antiquity. Only members of the official team are
allowed to dance or perform in public. But in spite of all
Church and folkloric restrictions, a touch of the old pagan
spirit usually sneaks into the collective soul. And away it
flies, free as all the winds of Provence.

Water, of symbolic significance since classical times, has to
be blessed by the first rays of the midsummer sunrise, which
gives it special healing powers. And from then on throughout
the day it is flung around in jugfuls, drenching as many people
as possible. Water pistols get into the act, and with these you
can always be sure of hitting your target.

Equally difficult for the folklore people to control is fire.
Dedicated to the god Belen, even the Church has trouble
in quelling its more rumbustious manifestations. Besides
which it still has its darker side, bringing back too many
burning memories of past inquisitions and not so distant
witch-hunts. However, the clergy have now managed to some
extent to curb the more frenzied cavortings connected with
fire worship.

In Vence it is the parish priest, surrounded by his vicars
and choirboys, who lights the fire of the fertility rites in front
of the church. Then comes the tarditional vine root shaped
like the woods of a stag, borne aloft by the chief male dancer
and placed in the middle of the bonfire. As the first flame
leaps up, the dancers spring into the fray, holding hands and
gambolling around the fire with *chevaux frus*, the dreaded
centaurs, galloping after them.

In the old days I remember sheep and donkeys being solemnly walked through the smoke, against fleas and the evil eye. Heads of garlic were pushed into the dying embers to ward off every kind of problem in the coming year, from thunder and lightning to carbuncles. By now, those quaint, rather embarrassing customs have been done away with.

After a scorching day, the night was hot and steamy. Mosquitoes droned around in squads. Doing their best, bats swooped out of the cypresses to scoop them up on the wing. Pierre, back at his barbecue, heaped thyme, sage and rosemary on the charcoal to create a thick anti-bug smoke.

By then the moonless sky was sparkling with stars, and our guests were beginning to arrive. Among them were Cindy and her exotic friend Herzi. Her husband had recently killed himself and, with his steadying influence gone out of her life, Cindy had lost her poise and all her hard-won serenity as well. As a result, she had gone back to her wild and distracted self of former days.

Her beautiful ash-blonde hair stood up round her head like a mad lion's mane. 'This is my disc-jockey gear,' she shrieked as she arrived, leaping about in a dervish suit of cream and chocolate satin.

Herzi looked stunning in black velvet tights, high-heeled shoes and silk shirt opened to the waist. A diamond necklace nestled in his chest fur and a large pearl dangled from his left ear on the end of a gold chain. Also there were our French journalist friend Daniel and his daughter, a famous model. She and Herzi, who had known each other in their *jeunesse dorée* in Paris, did a double-take. The last thing they expected was to meet again in this out-of-the-way *fête champêtre* in the foothills of the Alps. From then on, they were extremely cautious with each other, and I have often wondered what all that wariness concealed.

The other guests, friends of Alan's, were students at Nice University. One of them had found an African tom-tom in the dining room, and Nad was doing one of her 'liberated' dances to his drumming. Cindy, hair flying, spun round on one foot. Herzi leaped up and down on his high heels, and swung from branch to branch like Tarzan. Daniel's daughter, cool and inscrutable, watched their antics in silence. Her father, as urbane as ever, continued to converse in equable tones. The

German tenants, also invited to forestall trouble and complaints about the noise, must have thought they had landed
in some fearful kind of southern orgy. As they stared around
in stunned disbelief, I quickly filled their glasses and kept
them topped up.

Our bonfire, in the middle of the so-called lawn, was beginning to get out of hand. Taking off at the edges, little
golden flames were setting off on their own in various directions. It took all our precious Perrier water to put the whole
thing out. After that we lit a candle and planted it in the
grass. Our own symbolic bonfire. By then the surrounding
hills were ablaze with the rejoicings of shepherds and farmers, and the sound of flutes and Panpipes. No Folklore Committee could have kept down the routing and frolicking of
the old pagan spirit or the gambols of the mountain people
all firmly bent on enjoying themselves. The whole of Provence glittered that night with a million stars above, and fires
all over the land.

Breaking into the traditional rigadoon, we gambolled around
our candle's tiny flame. Nad, who would dearly have loved
to fling her skirts over her head, was thwarted by her harem
pants. We clapped in time to the tom-tom and chanted any
words that came into our heads. Round and round that silly
candle we hopped, until Pierre, the only one still sober among
us, shouted that dinner was ready. Sweating patiently over
the barbecue as usual, he had produced one more of his
delicious meals. Corks popped, glasses were refilled, and the
young settled down on the grass with their food. For us there
were tables and chairs. Herzi, who seemed unable to sit still,
kept leaping up and bouncing around, then taking another
swig. Was it only drink, I wondered, or was it drugs as well?
As for Cindy, she was in a strange, mutinous mood. I had
never seen her like that in her 'respectable' days.

After dinner Nad flew into the ring once more, with another
of her dervish dances. Charles stood up and did a solo ballet,
which looked like something out of Walt Disney's *Fantasia*.
Anne and I grabbed our shawls and twirled around him in a
complicated pattern which invented itself as we spun. Quite
unconcerned, the fireflies flickered in and out among us, intent
on their own affairs.

Suddenly we realized the noise had stopped. There was
no more drumming or shouting or laughing. The younger

element were standing still, staring goggle-eyed at our geriatric gyrations. Undaunted, we carried on, possessed by the spirits of the night.

Next morning, in spite of our nocturnal excesses, we were all up for breakfast. I mean, of course, the senior generation. The younger ones were nowhere to be seen. And when had Cindy and Herzi left?

We never saw Cindy again. A few weeks later, which she spent mostly in the nightclubs of Haut-de-Cagnes with Herzi, she took an overdose. The housekeeper found her slumped over a table in her hilltop house in Cagnes.

I saw Herzi once more, in Cindy's garden, when her ashes were being scattered over the flowerbeds she had tended so well during her husband's lifetime. Not long after came Herzi's own turn. Having tidied up his elegant mansion in the village, he had a bath and shave, then lay on his bed and slit his throat from ear to ear with an old-fashioned razor.

The night after our festivities a fearful explosion shook the house. My bed was rocking as I woke up. Echoes rolled and rumbled like thunder around the hills. 'Earthquake' shot through my head as I gripped the sheet to steady my nerves. The house finally stopped shuddering and the frogs, after being stunned into silence for a while, resumed their deafening racket.

It was some time before we discovered the cause of the explosion. A quarry in the Baou behind us had acquired a very large piece of machinery for crunching up rock into gravel-size pieces. This stone crusher, which had not yet gone into action, was the cause of much anxiety in the neighbourhood. Over a hundred local householders were quite happy to sign a petition declaring that the infernal machine wrecked the peace and quiet of the countryside, kept them awake at night and filled the air with dust – before it was even plugged in. Then came the bang, and up went the stone crusher, dynamited out of existence. The police came to inspect the damage, took fingerprints, sniffed the air and went home to consider. Some months later they had got no further. The insurers refused to pay as the contract was only valid once the machine was in action. As it had never been used . . .

The owner was desperate. Having borrowed the money to buy the appliance, he had no means of returning the loan.

Then one morning a man came to him with a proposition. For 5000 francs apiece, he was prepared to rub out any suspects and no questions asked. The deed would be done swiftly, with no suspicion ever pinned on anyone. 'The thing that amazed me most', the owner, Mr X, told me afterwards, 'was the incredibly low price quoted by the hit-man.'

Later on that summer the price was still the same. Once more in search of work, the would-be killer made the same proposition to Charles. Having delivered a load of paving stones for the garden, he brought up the subject out of the blue. As ignorant foreigners, he suggested, we would never know how to set about such matters. Most people have someone they want to rub out. If ever we were in that situation, he would be only too happy to oblige. Just in case, he left his card.

'Why so cheap?' I asked, puzzled.

'That's only the beginning,' said Charles. 'After that comes blackmail.'

CHAPTER 14

The Gates of Hell

ONE bright and sunny day not long after the midsummer festivities, we were lunching in the Millars' garden.

'I've got itchy feet,' said Joanna. 'Why don't we go off somewhere for a few days?'

'What a good idea. I don't see why not.'

'Where would you like to go?'

'Camargue,' I said, without hesitation.

The strange, mystery-ridden corner of Camargue, known to antiquity as the Gates of Hell, has intrigued me for as long as I can remember.

Two days later we were on the autoroute on our way to the west. After driving through miles of the huge white plain of Crau, we suddenly hit the first great lagoon of the area, the Etang de Berre, west of Marseilles. Leaving the motorway, we swung off to the right, across vast plains of reclaimed land and drained swamps, mostly planted with rice. Overhead cruised multitudes of kestrels, swooping down over the marshes in search of water birds and their nests.

As in days gone by, the land of Camargue is flooded in turn by the sea and by the waters of the Rhône. As a result, the area has developed a curious kind of plant life that enjoys both a salt- and fresh-water diet. Some of the animal and insect population, equally adapted to their surroundings, are found nowhere else in the world. And far more come in on migration than ever before, to raise their families in the huge nature reserve of Vaccarès in the north, the great draw of Camargue. The Delta, trapped between the two channels of the Rhône, is an enormous spongy triangle made up of floating rafts bristling with tangled reeds, roots and water plants.

Between these, constantly on the move, and swirling on currents and whirlpools, the sea drives its heavily salted waters into various parts of the swamp. Wherever possible, drains and canals bring in transfusions of fresh water to swill out the salt and prepare the soil for agricultural purposes. The scorching sun and desiccating winds bring to the light of day thick layers of salt and caked mud which crackle, split and explode in the punishing heat of noon. Ancient prehistoric and Roman fish hooks and harpoons constantly work their way to the surface of these ancient, crispy mud flats lying on top of layers of salt seven to ten metres deep. Two thousand years earlier, trade in smoked and pickled seafood had flourished in the area for the garum and other sauces made of rotting fish-gut to which the Romans were so addicted.

The enormous floating island of 62,500 hectares, built up by river debris over the ages, grows larger every year. Still said to be haunted, and full of legend, it is about one-third bigger now than when the Greeks arrived in Provence in about 600 BC. Growing roughly twenty to twenty-five metres larger each year, it pushes back the sea along the coast, all except in one place. At Saintes-Marie-de-la-Mer, the capital of world gypsyhood, the reverse is happening. Like some vast waste-disposal unit, the Mediterranean hits back, chewing away at the land and steadily gobbling it up in its mindless maw. The famous fortress church of Les Saintes, well inland when it was built in the Middle Ages, is now close to the sea and defended by powerful waterworks. The lighthouse at Faraman, starting its active life almost a mile inland in 1840, was swallowed up by the waves in 1917.

In the north, the lake of Vaccarès, which used to be brackish, has, through some mysterious process of its own, turned into fresh water. As a nature reserve, it is under the iron control of Tour du Vallat Scientific Station. No tourists are allowed anywhere near. In 1948 Luke Hoffman, vice-president of the World Wildlife Fund, first came to Camargue as a student. He bought Tour du Vallat and began to ring birds and study local plants and animals. But, most important of all, he imposed strict regulations for the protection of the area. Unfortunately not even these were enough to provide peace and quiet for the birds, whose nestlings are constantly traumatized by low-flying aircraft on their way in and out of Marignane airport. But in spite of this, Camargue is now regarded as the most important of all the wetlands of Europe and the only breeding ground of the pink flamingo. Another booming tribe of the area is the summer mosquito, which multiplies by the million in the reeking, stagnant waters of the marshes. Acting as a barrier between Vaccarès and the brackish lagoons of the south, the undisturbed prehistoric forest of Bois des Rièges is the only place in Europe where the Phoenician juniper grows, and the Asphodel, the Greek flower of the dead, shoots up to a height of over a metre. But most obtrusive of all is the overwhelming stench of the Stinking Yellow Everlasting. This aromatic wood, on the sea side, is the Sansouire, where the wild bulls and horses of Camargue come to feed. Paddling up to their knees in the sea-water swamps, they spend most of their lives grazing on their favourite fare, the spiky, arid Salicorne and Saladelle of the salt-water bogs.

The 88-kilometre sea dyke along which we were driving had become a hairline divide between the rushing river waters of the Rhône on one side, and the heavy waves of the brackish swamps on the other. With every gust of wind, a cascade of sea water flooded over the track, which disappeared from view and merged into one vast, heaving mass of lashing surf. A mad mistral howled over the swamps, blowing puffs of white scum across our bows. In the distance, on the horizon, a string of black bulls moved slowly along a dyke. Led by a couple of guardians on horseback, they all appeared to be walking on water.

Descended from the prehistoric aurochs, and living in the bogs as they do, these bulls have to be extremely tough to survive the ferocious climate of Camargue. Apart from the mistral, which brings hail and black frost, the Labech wind from south-south-west drives veritable cloudbursts and waterspouts inland from the sea. Entire herds of the graceful little black bulls are sometimes wiped out by these storms. But on the whole they are stout-hearted survivors. During particularly heavy gales, the bulls herd the cows into a pack and huddle closely round them in a circle facing out, breasting the full force of the wind until it abates or they fall down dead on the spot. Casualties are announced to the denizens of the area by the ramadan, a low rumbling roar which can be heard for miles around. With this eerie sound, the bulls bellow their grief to all the herds of Camargue.

Come the spring, the cows ramble off together to assist one another in the private business of procreation. All through the summer and following winter they stick together, keeping a close watch over their young. Soon after their first birthday, when the little bull calves emerge from their bogs, there is a nasty surprise for them. Their first brush with man brings them nothing but shock, pain and terror. This is when they are branded with their owners' initials. For these herds, wild and free though they seem, and believe themselves to be, all belong to *manadiers*, the bull farmers of Camargue.

As only one male can be kept in each herd, the next outrage imposed on the young bull is castration. But, surprisingly, this has no effect on the animal's high spirits and natural ferocity. By the time he is three, he is more than ready to prance into the ring to take part in the famous games. His agility, his liveliness and his strength are mightily respected by the *razeteurs*, who have to grab a rosette from his horns. Bright and sprightly, the little bull enters into the spirit of the game and thoroughly enjoys himself. He can size up a situation as quickly as any man and give his *razeteur* a good run for his money. He will even fly over the fence if the mood takes him and chase his man down the street for an extra thrill.

These light-footed bulls of Camargue, who specialize in the *course libre* (rosette-snatching game), are very different from their Spanish cousins. Smaller, far more nimble, they are swifter on the hoof, quicker-witted and much more loved and respected by one and all. As a result, unless they turn out to be downright cowards in the ring, they are never put to death. An even worse fate for a timid bull is to be sent to work in the fields, an indignity they find difficult to tolerate.

The frenzy of the bull feast is an unconscious throwback to the pagan days of the god Mithra, who stood for sun power and energy and whose cult was well established in Camargue long before the arrival of Christianity. In the branding ceremony, the *ferrade*, the guardian throws the animal to the ground by grabbing a horn and a front hoof. In these age-old movements and positions, man proclaimed his control over the brutish forces of the natural world. These rituals come right down from the original bull games of Minoan Crete. To seize the bull by the horns goes back a long way.

After the season in the ring is over, the guardians, on their unshod horses, lead the bulls back to the winter swamps.

Also escorting them are the *cavaliers*, a troop of fanatical amateurs, always far more numerous than necessary.

The trek through the marshes, lasting four or five days, is much enjoyed by the company, and the evenings around the camp fire are uproarious affairs. The *cavaliers* then return to civilization, but the guardians, armed with their tridents, stay alone in the bogs throughout the winter. Entirely dedicated to their animals, they regard themselves as a special breed, high priests of their bulls and horses, with traditions going back into the most distant past. More interested in honour, independence and freedom than in money, they are members of the Antique Confrérie de Taureaux et de Chevaux founded in 1520. St George is their patron and on his feast-day they set off decked out in glittering costumes, many of which have come down the centuries, saved from the teeth of moths and other calamities for almost five hundred years. They all meet in the Arles arena, where they plunge into fierce medieval jousts with javelins and lances and the lethal trident. Wielding all this formidable ironmongery, they thunder at one another, often crippling or killing a dear friend in the process.

On our way back along the flooded track, the wind was mercifully behind us. Splashing through the waves at a spanking pace, a string of white horses was heading north across the lagoon. Purposeful and determined, they seemed to know exactly where they were going. White from nose to tail and manes flying wildly in the wind, they were an intoxicating vision. But as they moved much faster than our water-logged vehicle, they were soon out of sight.

A little shaken by the fury of the elements, the car slowed down almost to a standstill. Joanna looked around doubtfully. 'I wonder if we should go on,' she muttered. 'If we break down here we've had it. Ooops . . .' she continued, as the car sprang into the air and we both hit the roof. 'I'm going on if it's the last thing I do,' she declared, stamping on the accelerator.

Breasting the flood, we shot forward with a mighty splash. The wind, growing wilder, seemed to be blowing from east and west at the same time. A huge wave swamped the windscreen. We were driving on water. 'This is the end of the world,' said Joanna appreciatively. And as the car bucked, bounced and cantered along the invisible track, the view began to change and the road narrowed. Suddenly a savage cloud of sand hit the car, blotting out everything in a screaming grey mist. We had reached the end of the dyke. From here, leaving its bed, the river thundered out to sea in total freedom. Straight ahead was an enormous beach of fine sand, most of which was racing through the air, carried up to cloud level by the gale.

Floating across the windscreen came the last thing anyone could ever have expected. Taking absolutely no notice of us, a large bare, pink human behind waddled past through the hissing sand. Several more followed. What could these nuts be doing, we wondered, prowling around in the nude in a raging sandstorm? It was then that we saw the sign: 'Naturist Reserve'.

One more conservation area in the land of protected species . . .

CHAPTER 15

The Soul of Provence

IN many ways, Provence has changed very little in the last thousand years or so. Faith, superstition, wishful thinking – who is to say where the line can be drawn? Alongside the official religion of the Roman Church, which they practise with some fervour, the peasants go on clinging to their ancient beliefs, which nothing has shaken so far. These are the well-tried facts they know about and that work for them on condition that the correct rites are duly observed. The Church is for the after-life, a kind of insurance for eternity, but it is of little help with daily pressing problems.

Until fairly recently life was still very hard for the people of Provence and particularly for the peasants. As there were few doctors outside the towns, most outlying farms and vineyards were out of reach of medical help. Until well after the last war, the telephone was unknown. As a result, by the time a horse-cart had trundled off to collect help, the patient might well be dead. And so, over the centuries, these tough, hard-working, uncomplaining people evolved their own ways of dealing with most emergencies, accidents and other hazards. Almost every village still has its healer and usually a genuine witch as well.

Some of the healing methods I remember from childhood days now seem outlandish and bizarre. Among the remedies I have come across were several for bedwetters, who could be cured of their shameful weakness by swallowing a brew made of dried powdered mouse or keeping a live toad under the bed. Burns treated with grated raw potatoes healed very quickly. Cataract was cured with drops of squashed snail juice and scraped cuttlefish bone. Raw beef applied to a black eye worked miracles overnight. Chilblains were eased with red wine and celery juice. And you could avoid them altogether by carrying a turnip in your pocket as a preventive. The following specific for colds and bronchitis was still in use in the fifties and perhaps even now. Working again with the handy snail, squash a few of them, shells and all, sprinkle with sugar and leave to soak overnight. Swallow the resulting brew and all symptoms vanish within a few hours. As for herbal potions they are so numerous and often so contradictory that I will mention only a few. The list is particularly long for insomnia. Lime blossom is, of course, a classic, and so is lettuce, as Peter Rabbit found to his cost. Poppies are notorious for their hypnotic virtues and hawthorn unexpectedly effective. As for marjoram, I already knew about it. Or so I thought.

As I was going through a period of acute insomnia, I decided to try that one out myself. Although it worked quite well to start with, the effect wore off, and I had to increase the dose. After a couple of days, I found it difficult to get out of bed in the morning, and even to find the floor, which seemed to be swivelling about all over the room. Standing up was even worse. Clutching the walls, I could hardly make out which way I was going. By the end of the week I woke up to such a fit of the staggers that I thought I must have had a stroke. Out of curiosity, I checked my herb book again and there, right at the end of the chapter, the last sentence pointed out that taken in heavy doses, marjoram can induce catalepsy. So much for marjoram.

Before the war, diphtheria was a dread and nearly always fatal affliction, for which no treatment was known at the time. A string of garlic hanging round the neck was the only thing which the distracted parents could do for their dying child. Some added a picture of St Blaise for good measure (he had been strangled to death in an iron collar). Epidemics of all kinds were rampant, and it was a case of survival of the fittest.

In Vence, that well-known centre of folk medicine, a high fever was usually cured by placing a toad, as poison absorber, under the bed. If it failed to work, the creature was boiled with herbs and the broth swallowed by the patient. Sometimes chewing a few live spiders could help as well. But when all else failed, you propped up the patient against a

peach tree, the complaint was transferred, and the tree died
as a result. Insanity was cured with a branch of hypericum or
tufts of juniper under the patient's pillow, and this prevented
baldness as well. Meningitis was a terror and nearly always
fatal, even when treated with a pigeon cut in half and wrapped,
still warm, around the patient's head. For paralysis you drank
tobacco juice or covered the soles of your feet with salt and
fetched a goat to lick it off. Pneumonia was usually fatal.
Sometimes a dose of wine, olive oil and spices was administered
or an inverted glass, stuffed with a wad of burning cotton
wool, was clamped to the chest. The blue swelling the size
of a golf ball, which appeared after the glass was wrenched
off, sometimes had a cross slashed into it to let out the poison.

Concocting love potions has always been an intriguing subject. In the old days, the more bizarre the ingredients, the
more effective they proved. Maurice Messegué, that high priest
of the herb world, recommends cow parsnip, mint, fenugreek,
celandine and garlic as reliable aphrodisiacs. Savory and rocket,
his last two suggestions, are so powerful that medieval monks
were forbidden to grow them in their monastery gardens.

There are a great many recipes for love philtres, but as
hot-blooded Southerners are seldom in need of them I have
come across very few in these parts.

Kidnapping was a constant fear for parents and children
in those pre-war days. As a very real danger, it was a
terror to the young. One much-publicized case was that of
a boy stolen by gypsies, drugged and made to 'prophesy'
in the fairground. Others were trained as clowns or acrobats
or sold in Marseilles for Moorish harems or the slave trade.
In one way and another, children had a tough time. Roughly
fed and made to work hard, they were often ill, as they
usually caught everything that was going. But once they
succumbed, no trouble was too great to get them well again.
Ill health being a national hobby, the case was taken up
by the neighbourhood and every suggestion put to the test.
One I remember well was treatment for whooping cough.
An almost infallible cure was to push the little patient back
and forth seven times under the belly of a donkey.
Unfortunately not all donkeys had the gift. There were only
a few specialists, each one well known in the province.
And to these the afflicted would be driven, bumping along
in a horse-cart over the rough stony tracks, through miles

of vineyards and olive groves. Altogether, the precarious journey through life from birth to death had to be protected by magic rites of ancient and well-tried practice. As the Church was not able to winkle out such deep-rooted beliefs, it wisely absorbed some of the more harmless ones and converted them to Christianity.

There are many villages where processions for rain still take place with fireworks, banners, hymns and holy statues but no longer with the help of the clergy. In Châteauneuf there reigns a Madonna whose rain-producing powers never fail. Every time she travels in procession across the vines with the faithful, they are soaked to the bone if they set off without umbrellas. Her chapel, built over a pagan shrine, has been the rain centre for the whole region for over two thousand years.

When sunshine is required to ripen the grapes, the needs of the fields go into reverse and rain must be kept at bay. Until Vatican II stamped out the practice, it was the local priest's duty to send the storm growling over to the next village. If this failed to work, he threw his shoes at the sky and the desired results followed. But if the next-door priest was equally gifted in storm control, a good thunderstorm could be kept rumbling back and forth between the two parishes for several hours.

Hail, so disastrous for the harvest, is dissolved in many ways. You can either throw salt at it, or plant knives in the soil, pointing at the sky, ring church bells or blast off rockets. These, which can be heard booming around the Baous throughout the summer, are regarded as the best hail-control method at the moment. One of these heavy rockets landed in our garden one morning, fortunately too early to brain anyone as it crashed to the ground.

Another heathen practice that had been duly christianized was the blessing of the crops in the fields. This I well remember watching as a child. The endless processions, headed by priests and choirboys swinging incense, snaked along the dusty tracks, with the great Cross swaying from side to side, blessing the fruits of the earth. It was the astute St Césaire of Arles who converted the pagan 'Balationes', rites of Cybele, into the Christian 'Rogations' of the Roman Church. Nowadays it is a very different affair. Organized in a theatrical way, it has totally lost the original reverence and wholehearted faith of former days. Conducted by the Folklore Committee, the Rogation festival now takes place in the fields north of Vence around the old chapel of St Columba.

As the fertility rites were often too crude for conversion, they were mostly ignored. Only one, as far as I know, has survived. Until a few years ago, at the little church of St Rolain, a noted fertility saint, there was a constant tinkle of pale pink male organs, made of painted tin, spinning round the altar. The objects, hanging from the tabernacle on a thread, waltzed and jingled in the faintest breeze. In the end, distracted by the constant chiming during the services, the priests asked for the objects to be made of some soft material, instead of tin. The change was duly made, and all was well for a time. Then came Vatican II, and new, stern measures were enforced. The little amulets had to be cut down, and they now lie, silent and unseen, packed away in shoe boxes around the altar.

In the Middle Ages holy relics and the bones of saints were in great demand. This gave rise to profitable trading in pig and chicken bones, while the tombs of saints were in constant danger from grave robbers.

With the Vatican Council and the New Look, superstition has been suppressed wherever possible. But other harmless manifestations such as processions in the streets, banners, incense, rogations, open-air masses, done away with as well, are much regretted by the faithful.

As I drove about in the depths of the countryside, the first thing I did on reaching a new village was always to call on the parish priest for general information about the area. This was a revelation. Remembering the long-robed, rosy-cheeked and chubby prelates of the old days, I was stunned to be met on many a presbytery doorstep by earnest, stern-looking young priests with haunted eyes, dressed in turtleneck sweaters and skin-tight jeans. These dedicated young disciples were ruthlessly cutting out all the trimmings that had so comfortably accumulated over the centuries. As a result of this new decree, isolated villages and mountain people, bereft of their mystical rites and ceremonies, turned to magic and witchcraft. And the priests of the New Look are now having trouble reclaiming and delivering the faithful from the error of their ways, so that country police records are filled with reports and complaints of 'damage by witchcraft'.

Even in Nice there is a cabal which meets regularly in sinister seclusion. These Satanists are killers, or so they believe. A report in *Nice-Matin* described a ritual murder to which they lay claim. There is quite a number of these occult groups all over Provence. But the Cult of Satan is a very different affair.

The young man who runs the show complains of being unpopular with the locals, who do not understand what he is up to. According to him, his god and master Lucifer, the Angel of Darkness who lights up the night, is actually a cosmic emanation coming from Venus. 'I teach people to sublimate their animal instincts into a subtle force, which helps them to self-knowledge,' babbles this exotic young man with mad-looking eyes. At the age of seven he had his first 'astral trip'. Sent early to boarding school, he would wing his way home in his astral body to spy on his parents. When he told them later what they had been up to, they began to worry. What was this strangeling they had engendered?

Living in a hut in the mountains, he felt too exposed to his enemies and moved to a secret cave further up, where he worships his master with a group of dedicated disciples. But the outcome of the initiating rites is not always successful. Occasionally the candidate to spiritual awakening dies of fright during the ceremony. What happens then?

'Well,' said the high priest sadly, 'the police regard it as murder. They don't know any better. It is just one of the trials of transmigration that we have to endure. But', he added more firmly, 'the time for superstition is over. A proper scientific centre for the study of our practices should open very shortly.'

Needless to say, nothing of the kind has happened, nor is ever likely to do so.

CHAPTER 16

The Black Death

DURING my trips around the countryside I kept hearing about an *ancien village* tucked away, nobody knew exactly where, deserted since the Middle Ages and still a total ruin. I quizzed every mayor and parish priest I came across and eventually discovered where the village was supposed to be.

Early one summer morning, Anne and I set off on our way north. The road, clamped in horrific hairpin bends against the side of a perpendicular alp behind Nice, was much worse than we had bargained for. As we crept round the V-shaped bends, carefree French drivers came screeching down the mountain on two wheels. Finally, after negotiating the last bend, we reached a high plateau tucked away behind our vertical peak. Here, at the top of the world, the air was so clear that you could see as far as the next stretch of highlands, the massive range of the true Alps in the distance, still shrouded in snow. There is something extraordinarily, wondrously heady and exhilarating about the air and the feeling of static, timeless tranquillity of a mountain top. Perhaps it has something to do with getting there in one piece.

Feeling light-headed and slightly dazed, we stared around us as a couple of magpies came hopping up to inspect us more closely, and find out what strange new animals had invaded their territory. Squinting first with one unbelieving eye, they whipped round to check up with the other. After which, with squawks of disapproval, they flapped away together.

It was up here that we found the *ancien village*. Almost overwhelmed by the wild vegetation of the mountain, the old fortress town stands on the tip of a high rocky spur overlooking the valley 700 metres below. And, way beyond, the sea gleams like some vast slab of white metal.

Leaving the car on the plateau, we climbed up to the citadel, a huge area that must have been a sizeable town with heavy defensive walls and which in no way could be described as a village. It was more than likely that no one had seen it for a very long time and it had become a legend in the minds of the local population.

The church, which had lost its steeple, was unbelievably battered, a complete ruin. Surrounded by massive ramparts and crumbling towers, the site had obviously been a large and prosperous fortified city. From the very top of the spur, the view took in the plain below and the two valleys on either side, through which trickle the first rains of the season. Over the centuries these two canyons had been the habitual highways of invading Barbarians, Saracens and assorted bandits of all kinds and races. How could such devastation have occurred? Judging by other similar ruins I had seen all over Provence, it appeared to date from the eleventh or twelfth century at the latest. Impregnable as it was on top of its rock, the town could only have been defeated by an epidemic of the plague. Knights on their way back from the Crusades, straying monks, visiting troubadours, any of them could have arrived, crawling with plague fleas, which instantly infected the entire population. La Gaude and St Laurent du Var are just two other examples of a similar fate.

This plague, which racked Europe for so many centuries, was a complete mystery to the people of the time. The theories about its cause and origins were as wild as they were numerous. People had no idea where it came from. Anything unusual or unexpected could be held responsible, if an outbreak occurred soon after. Ignorance, panic and superstition led people to believe whatever they heard, however improbable. To begin with, the stars were held responsible. Comets appearing during an epidemic would take all the blame. One of them, particularly large and terrifying, called for public prayers to keep panic at bay. Solemnly excommunicated by the Pope, it lost some of its terror. But it was Halley who finally defused the trauma by correctly predicting its periodic reappearance.

The Church put it all down to the sins of humanity. In France, the royal family were blamed for letting some of their children marry within forbidden degrees of relationship. In England the bishops claimed it was caused by the theatre,

and in Spain it was put down to the opera. And everywhere
the clergy thundered against the long pointed shoes which
curled upward in wanton defiance of Heaven.

Originating in China, and travelling along the Silk Road, the
Black Death devastated Europe and the Middle East for several hundred years. Twenty-five million Europeans, or 90 per
cent of the population, perished of the sickness. The disastrous view that washing and bathing were sinful, and likely
to bring on the disease, was the cause of its lightning spread.
Lack of hygiene was the bane of the Middle Ages. Filth accumulated in living quarters, open drains ran through the streets,
and rats wallowing in piles of rotting garbage spread their
lethal plague-ridden fleas in all directions. These killer rats
had originally sailed to Europe with returning Crusaders. There
were actually two varieties of infection, the bubonic and the
pneumonic. With the first, the disease settled in the lymph
glands, which swelled up, causing terrible pain. Black boils,
high fever and coma came next, soon followed by death.

Even more deadly was the pneumonic variety, which filled
the lungs with blood. Pole-axed by rocketing fever, coughing
and spitting blood, the victims succumbed within a few hours.
The afflicted soon became convinced they could shake off the
disease by passing it on to someone else, which led to delib-
erate mutual infection, particularly of pet hates and enemies.
Another way of handing it on was by 'greasing' and 'smear-
ing' the neighbours' doors and belongings. Witches, who encouraged their clients in this habit, even sold home-made
plague poison for eliminating enemies. 'Plague scarers' were
caught dropping 'plague worms' into holy water in church.
There was also a brisk trade in spiders, toads and lizards for
soaking up the poison.

'The venomous tongues of snakes worn close to the body
are very good,' said Paracelsus, who should have known
better. In 1348 the Medical Faculty in Paris said no fowl,
fish or old beef should be eaten at all. Exercise was lethal.
And woe betide those who slept in a woman's bed. As for
baths, nothing could have been more wicked. The Church
totally opposed scientific experiment, research or medical
investigation. The Popes banned post-mortems, and all
anatomical study was forbidden.

It was the lower ranks of the clergy who showed the
greatest devotion to the sick. Heroic in their selflessness,

they staggered along in the throes of their own agony to take the last sacraments to the dying. Some holy orders specialized in burying the dead, while others nursed the sick in hospitals. Meanwhile the Church amassed great wealth with enormous donations from the victims who were hoping to buy their way into Heaven.

Surprisingly, the Middle Ages were unusually well organized in charity and welfare work. As the dedicated souls who went in for this kind of work were kind and compassionate, the atmosphere was full of brotherly love and devotion. There are contemporary prints showing grand bewimpled ladies arranging flowers under the marvelling eye of half a dozen naked men, all tucked up together in one enormous bed.

Avignon was almost wiped out by the plague, after which it was the turn of Marseilles, the victim of an appalling disaster.

On its way back from the East with a cargo of infected rats, the Grand Saint Antoine unloaded its treasures with a falsified health certificate, which claimed that the great number of deaths on board during the voyage were due to food poisoning. And so the polluted rats and passengers were unloaded with the blessing of the authorities. Within a week people were dropping dead in their tracks all over the town. In no time the prosperous city was turned into a reeking charnel house with corpses piling up everywhere, heaving with worms and liquefying in the terrible heat of August. The stench was appalling, and the air unbreathable. Then came a great wind which cleared the atmosphere and blew the bugs far and wide, thus spreading the infection all over the land.

Nice lost 8000 citizens in one year. Grasse, Antibes, Mougin, Châteauneuf, Cagnes, Villeneuve, St Paul were all burying their dead. Vence, taking ruthless precautions, avoided disaster. All 'foreigners' were thrown out of town, and nobody was allowed through the gates. Refugees who came begging for food were beaten back by the militia. On the threat of flogging, no one was allowed to cross the Loup or the Var rivers.

The Jews alone were surprisingly little affected by the epidemics. Their high degree of immunity was a constant puzzle to the Christians. With their better understanding of hygiene, Jewish communities avoided the water of wells and rivers. But when they did succumb, they usually recovered through the selfless nursing of their families. This was another mystery to the Christians, who usually fled at the first sign of danger, deserting husbands, wives and children to save their own skins.

Soon, a few simple souls, questioned on the rack, admitted to seeing Jews drop little bags of worms into open wells. And this was the start of another of these mindless and infamous persecutions.

Totally fear-ridden, these were terrible times, with every form of evil flourishing on all sides. Terror and hysteria reigned. All normal civilization came to an end. Famine followed, with other diseases in tow, such as flu, tuberculosis, scurvy and leprosy. Wolves prowled around the streets and dragged children out of their beds. Carrion birds pecked at rotting corpses. Order and decency vanished. Crime was rampant. 'Dance of Death' paintings with men, women and demons all cavorting together, often stark naked, appeared everywhere. One of these, in a perfect state of preservation, hangs in the church in Bar-sur-Loup.

CHAPTER 17

The Lakes of Hell

As June is the month when the high valleys of the Alps are at their best and wild flowers are out in their millions, I decided to go up to 'Val des Merveilles' before the mountain plants began to wilt. Would anyone come with me? I asked hopefully. But the family, crushed by the heat and their unending toil in the garden, made endless excuses. So I set off on my own, and that is how I came to join a party of scientists from an archaeological society in Nice.

'Meraviglie' is how a seventeenth-century Italian historian described the prehistoric rock engravings in the Alps, high above the little frontier town of Tende. When the area became French after the last war, the Italian word, which had stuck, was translated into 'Merveilles', in the sense of 'extraordinary, amazing wonders'. That is why the long narrow cleft 6000 metres up in the Mercantour mountain range of the Alps at the foot of Mount Bego, where the rock carvings appear, is known as 'Val des Merveilles'.

By joining the Nice scientists on their trip to the mountains in their battered old bus, I thought I would learn from them all I could possibly want to know on the subject. But as they discussed nothing but their innumerable ailments throughout the journey, and the carvings were not even mentioned, I dropped my experts as soon as we reached the end of the road. They climbed into jeeps, and I pounded off along the track towards the mountain face. There the Alp rose sheer, like a stone wall covered with loose stones and jutting rocks. Water, ice-cold from the melting snow above, flowed down in sheets. On hands and knees I began to scramble up this streaming rockface and within minutes

I was drenched to the skin. I slithered on the sodden moss, grabbing at rocks and roots. Finally, after much backsliding, I reached the top, and there, lying dead still under Heaven, were the pewter-coloured waters of the first of the Lakes of Hell. This one, the Devil's first-born, was 'Le Lac du Diable'.

Hoping to keep the faithful away from the pagan area, the Church had proclaimed it to be a haunt of demons, a centre of evil and witchcraft. But psychologically, it was a bad move. The opposite effect was achieved. Intrigued and attracted by all the mystery, the still, dark lakes and the magical beauty of the mountain top, people have been flocking to the high valley ever since.

Cautiously I set off along the soggy, slippery edge of the Devil's Lake. Shepherds and their entire flocks have been sucked into its depths, never to be seen again. Severely bewitched, these lakes never give up their secrets. Left behind by the last ice age, they are frozen solid for most of the year. The Lakes of Hell all lie in the path of the great glacier, the last to dissolve in the southern Alps eight thousand years ago. Beyond the long stretch of still waters is the famous cleft of polished rock on which were scratched the famous figures I had come to see.

And there as well, alas, were my experts, swarming and twittering like excited sparrows. So off I sped to the other end of the rift, where all was quiet and peaceful. At this height we were level with the top of the range. The air was so sharp and clear that it practically tinkled. The whole sky, a deep Meissen blue, was rimmed by the dazzling white peaks of the Alps. Patches of snow lay over the short grass, and everywhere wild flowers poked through wherever they could. Marmots, sitting up like teddy-bears on their doorsteps, whistled angrily at my approach. Water gushed everywhere. The rumble of torrents came from all directions. Above the tree-line, at this height, there is nothing but rock and water. The famous valley had the look of a rock garden covered with pictures shrouded in mosses and lichens. Forty thousand of these figures have already been cleaned up and exposed to view, mostly sketches of bulls and goats and weird men with legs growing out of their heads, all marching along the rockface in a lively, endless frieze. Further down were daggers, lances, scythes, ploughshares. Mysterious shapes and designs, probably magic signs, appeared here and there. One menacing figure, known as the Sorcerer, had daggers tied to his wrists.

Peering down into the valley 6000 metres below, you could see tiny square fields dotted with pigmy cows, exact replicas of the carved strip along the rockface at our level.

It was Clarence Bicknell, an English clergyman living in Bordighera, who first unravelled this wild tangle of pre-Christian art. Soon after discovering the prehistoric site, he built himself a chalet in Casterino and spent the last eighteen years of his life dedicated to the rockface engravings, of which he made 1400 casts. Carlo Conti, an Italian sculptor, took over after Bicknell's death. From 1927 to 1942, Conti hauled tons of plaster up the mountain on mule-back, to carry on with the castings.

Experts believe that the valley was a cult centre for Mount Bego, the Lord of the Range, the magic mountain that dominates the surroundings with such awesome majesty. Even modern archaeologists admit to being impressed by its aura. And to the shepherds of five thousand years ago who came up to graze their animals on the high pastures, Bego was positively godlike. With his head always above cloud level, and radiating a kind of impassive power and authority, he filled them with fear and reverence.

After pecking at the rockface from end to end of the rift, my experts finally passed a solemn resolution to protect the site from thieves and vandals 'on account of its inestimable value for the study of mankind'. And after this grandiose pronouncement, they retreated to their various haunts, feeling they had done great things for the human race.

A couple of weeks later, having coerced a few friends into joining me, we tackled the mountain again, this time from the north-east. Starting from Casterino, we hired a couple of jeeps and made for the high valley of Fontanalba. From this angle, Bego stood to the south, sharp and clear above his usual collar of ballooning cloud.

On the way to the top we stopped at Clarence Bicknell's house, a plain wooden chalet next to a cascading torrent, surrounded on all sides by the chirping of birds in the fir trees, the whistling of marmots among the rocks, clouds of butterflies zig-zagging over thick patches of wild flowers and the white peaks of snow-covered Alps in the distance. It was here that Bicknell wrote his many books on the flowers and ferns of the region and *A Guide to the Prehistoric Rock*

Engravings in the Italian Maritime Alps, all of which are now recognized classics of the region.

Back in our jeeps we veered off sharply to the left, up a steep track fit only for goats and mules. Spread out over the mountainside was a herd of cows nibbling the juicy grass, watched over by a melancholy donkey loaded with the shepherd's luggage, his cat and a supply of snake-bite serum, much needed in these parts.

Come the spring thaw, and forbidden by law to keep their flocks and herds in the plain after a certain date, farmers drive their animals up to the high pastures at the beginning of June. This, which takes place in three stages, follows the retreating snow-line. Finally, as summer comes to an end, singing and yodelling, the assembled cowherds return to their village to the sound of church bells and mouth organs. The best milch cow of the season wears flowers in her horns, and the girls dance around her much as they did in the days of the wild rock-carving mountain tribes. The cattle (or would 'kine' be more apt?) spend the winter in warm, smelly quarters beneath the family chalet in the village.

I asked our driver how the herdsmen spend their time during the summer weeks, under the open sky twenty-four hours on end.

'Well, obviously, living close to the world of nature as they do, they get to know a lot about plants, including all their medicinal and magic properties,' he said.

'Do they use the plants to treat themselves and their animals?'

'Yes, apart from the snake serum, that's all they use up here, just plants and roots.'

'And what about magic?'

'Well, they know how to chase thunderstorms away from their herds and dissolve heavy mists to protect their animals from pneumonia and also how to frighten away evil spirits with their fierce piping. And when someone dies in the valley, they can see the soul floating past on its way to Heaven or Hell.'

It is shepherds who brew love potions for the local lads. A good one, our driver told me, was a mixture of achilleia, gentian and hyssop. But when I asked him for the proportions, he changed the subject.

On the whole it is not surprising that these herdsmen are held in such awe by the people of the plains. Standing stark and gaunt like a scarecrow outlined against the sky, on top of a rocky spur, a shepherd in full rig is an impressive sight.

Wrapped in his vast hooded cloak flapping around his donkey-hide boots, he looks like some menacing medieval demon casting spells to all corners of the world.

The very top of Fontanalba was as smooth as a golf links and covered with myriad wild flowers. There were orchids, bright pink daphnes, edelweiss, genista like great patches of fluid gold, the delicate white blossom of Alpine tea, poppies, dwarf forget-me-nots and thousands more that none of us could identify. Rose of the Alps, the tiny mountain rhododendron, grew everywhere, favourite food of the local grouse. Its dark red blossom is like wide rivers of blood pouring down the surrounding slopes. But most profuse of all was the deep, intense blue of the gentians, which grew as thick as carpet-pile in all directions, as far as you could see.

Solar radiation, which increases sharply with altitude, puts a tremendous strain on all these flowering plants, as well as adding an enamel gleam, and a great intensity, to all the colours. A smooth green slope will turn into a brilliant tapestry, with thousands of flowers appearing overnight on stalks which did not exist the day before. But in spite of all their problems – icy winds, melting snows, floods, killer sunlight and heavy soggy mists – Alpine plants win the battle every time and seem quite contented with their lot.

Hobbling and tottering over the rocks to Lac Vert, we clattered down into Valmasque, the Valley of the Witch, the actual bed of the old ice-age glacier, where we climbed back into our jeeps. As we crashed about among the rocks of the moraine the driver told us that the glacier began to break up fifteen thousand years ago at the end of the last ice age. Altogether it had taken eight thousand years to dissolve, and along the sides of this valley, on the smooth polished stone left in its wake, prehistoric men also carved their figures at the time.

'But not just any rock, mind you,' said our incredibly learned man. 'It had to be green or purple schist, covered with a layer of red iron oxide.'

And he turned us out of our vehicles to inspect the work at close quarters. The ancient tribes, our man went on, believed that the earth swallowed up the sun every night and coughed it up again in the morning to light up the magic mountain, which could then be worshipped once more throughout the day.

As the sun was now in the west, the floodlit rocks all

round were a staggering sight of glowing pink, ochre, geranium red and cadmium yellow, according to the structure and formation of each crag. Inevitably, a place of this kind breeds legends. There is a story of a young shepherd, about a hundred years ago, who decided to go and investigate the nature of the glowing fire that blazed on the magic mountain every morning. So one night he set off by the light of the moon, leaving his dog to watch over the dozing flock. Climbing steadily, he finally arrived next day at sunset. As he looked around for a comfortable spot for the night, he tripped and tumbled off the topmost ridge of the great mountain. Bouncing from rock to rock, he crashed all the way down to the bottom 700 metres below. When the shepherds gathered at their regular meeting place to set off down the mountain at the end of the summer, they realized that one of their colleagues was missing. They waited as long as they could, but finally had to leave when the first snow began to fall. A few weeks later they saw the missing flock appear, led by a girl who looked exactly like the missing shepherd. All she could tell them was that she had fallen off the top of Mount Bego and described the exact spot where she crashed at the bottom. When they all went to visit the place the following summer, a new spring suddenly gushed out of the rock at their feet, and the surroundings were instantly covered with flowers. But there was no sign of the young shepherd anywhere, and the girl continued to look after his sheep.

Valmasque also has its story. After the local witch had been banished to the mountains by the Lord of Tende, the people of the town forgot about her, all but a young shepherd from Saorge who decided to go and find out what she was up to. Leading his flock into the Valley of Hell, he vanished, and nothing was heard from him again. Years later, his bones, and those of the sheep, were discovered at the bottom of one of the lakes. It was named Saorgina in memory of the foolish young man who should have known better. A group of monks was dispatched in due course to bless and exorcise the spot. No sooner had they arrived than flights of ravens swarmed around, trying to peck out their eyes. Most of the birds were instantly turned into trees, and the few who escaped the curse of the monks fled to Val des Merveilles. And there you can see them to this day, forever cruising overhead but never allowed to land, demons every one of course.

CHAPTER 18

The Season

By midsummer, 'the season' was in full swing and the international community along the coast was leading a busy social life.

With Florence at El Patio in Cannes, and Dolly up on the heights at Les Valettes, Diana and Jimmy at Val Romey in Antibes and Helen at Elen Roc, next to Hôtel du Cap, not to speak of the 'International Set' in Monte Carlo, there was a non-stop round of dinner parties all through the summer.

It was in the twenties that the new 'out-of-season' craze was launched by a young American who gave a 4th of July party, persuading the owner of Hôtel du Cap to stay open at the end of a long and busy winter period. This was the start of an even more popular craze. From then on, 'the season' switched from the previous winter months to the long, hot summer of the Riviera.

In 1926, Florence's husband had launched the Hôtel Provençal at Juan-les-Pins, which had been totally unknown until then. There, he was soon entertaining his friends, with the help of Harpo Marx, Somerset Maugham, Douglas Fairbanks, the Murphys and a fizzing young divorcee named Wallis Simpson.

Soon after her husband's death, Florence moved to El Patio, a large and comfortable villa by the sea just outside Cannes. This house, which she consolidated into a fortress, was soon filled with a priceless collection of paintings and many other treasures. When the famous robbery took place, the burglars climbed on the roof, removed a few tiles and got in without trouble. But meanwhile Florence entertained her friends throughout the summer.

Totally uninterested in social gossip, Dolly gathered prominent writers and journalists around her table, both in Cannes
and in London. As a salon Socialist, she included a selection
of top Labour politicians as well. I was once placed beside
Harold Wilson, and I regret to say that neither of us much
enjoyed the experience.

Next door to Hôtel du Cap, Helen's château stood on a
rocky spur overlooking the sea. We spent many happy days
lying on her private beach, swimming in the bay and enjoying
lazy picnics under the palm-thatch awning she had built
against the cliff.

And suddenly, without warning, this blissful life came to an
end. As a Swiss resident, Helen paid the normal tax for foreigners
who lived abroad and visited their French property only for a
few weeks in the year. Somehow the local authorities became
aware of the enormous value of the estate, and a huge tax
claim was made out of the blue. Poor Helen, shattered by
the unexpected blow, retired to Switzerland for good and
presented the town with the whole place, château, land,
private beach and coastline as a private gift in perpetuity.
She died soon after this – of a broken heart, I shouldn't
wonder.

The private beach at La Garoupe was reserved for the
film stars and celebrities staying at the hotel opposite. There,
Anne Behar told me that she often saw the Oliviers, the
Attenboroughs and many others with their families and their
guests.

I just remember Sir Duncan Orr-Lewis, a much-married
Canadian baronet and the life and soul of the French Riviera.
He had built several villas along the coast and lived at
Duncanna by the time we met him. It was, in fact, his
mother who had sold El Patio to Florence.

On our way back from these soirées along the coast, Charles
and I always stopped in Vence to visit the baker in his lair
and buy our breakfast bread straight out of the great brick
oven that roared away all through the night. It was like
stepping back five hundred years in time. In his white vest
and shorts, and a paper hat on his head, he was covered
with flour from head to foot.

I often wondered why, even at the hottest time of the
year, the baker always kept his door firmly closed. We

had to slink through a crack, and the portals were instantly slammed behind us. It is only quite recently that I discovered the reason for this. Water, flour and leaven, which make up bread, have been considered magic elements since the beginning of time. Filled with occult powers, they have to be handled with care and respect. While the loaves, particularly vulnerable to spells and curses, are still in the oven, the baker must never speak to anyone on his doorstep. Once inside, visitors who are no longer a threat to the bread in the oven, can stay and prattle as long as they like. Our baker was always quite happy to entertain his guests till dawn, when he normally went home to breakfast. But until then there was no stopping the flow.

First came a rundown on the family's health, with Madame's problems at the top of the list. As one of the best cooks in Vence, she obviously enjoyed her own cuisine, which unfortunately all ran to fat. On one occasion, at the beginning of June, together with all the neighbours, I was there to cheer her on her fiftieth wedding anniversary. Dressed in pink organdie, she had no trouble getting through her front door with the aid of a stick, and we helped to ease her into the family car, as the whole tribe set off to celebrate at their favourite restaurant up in the mountains. So much for Madame.

Next on the bulletin came the state of her brother's health. Known as *'le chauffeur'*, he pushed the bread to market at dawn in an old basket on wheels and suffered from unquenchable nosebleeds. Advised to consume fewer glasses of wine each day, he had duly cut down on the number but increased the size of the glasses. To his surprise and chagrin, his condition had not improved.

Our baker, who had been training his son-in-law over the past twenty years, never liked to leave him alone at night.

'Three thousand loaves is too much for him all on his own,' he would say. 'Too much for a novice on his own.'

Well into his seventies, the old boy was still doing a full night's work. After the flour, leaven and water had been mixed in the old kneading trough, the loaves were shaped, then lined up on long, supple, wooden paddles. Taking a razor blade from his teeth, Son-in-Law made a few quick slits on each lump of dough, then the paddle was carefully

inserted into the brick oven. Shaking it free, he dropped
the loaves into their appointed places.

The oven, beyond its minute opening, was as vast as the
bakery itself. Five hundred loaves fitted into it in one go.
The baker knew exactly where each one was, how long it
had been in, and when it was ready to come out. Every
few seconds, the paddle would shoot in like a snake's tongue,
to pick up one single loaf somewhere in the depths of the
glowing oven. Crisp and crackling and too hot to touch, it
was rolled on the sideboard next to all the others, the
right way up. Only the public executioner's bread was ever
laid upside down.

When the bread came out of the oven limp and flaccid,
the baker would announce in gloomy tones, 'It's going to
rain tomorrow.'

'How do you know?' we always asked.

'Crisp bread needs a clear sky.'

I once inquired about the wood used to make these long
supple paddles forever shooting in and out of the blazing
oven and yet never getting scorched. Was it Bo, or Itm, or
Almug, or Sissoo wood, or something even more exotic?
But our baker had no idea. He was not concerned with
paddle wood, only with his bread, for which he had received
many prizes, had featured in a book and appeared on
television.

To break the monotony of the long nights, he enjoyed
doing extra jobs. Knowing, as he claimed, that nobody can
eat English bread, he always produced an outsize loaf for
Charles whenever he went to London. As large as a bicycle
wheel and solid right through, it was so heavy I could
hardly lift it. 'This will last a month,' our baker would
declare. 'It will keep you going until you come back.' At
which I had visions of Charles stepping past the porter at
his London club with his loaf under his arm.

Our baker had the air and majesty of a grandee as he
handed over his massive gift. We knew, and he knew that
we knew, how much care, pride, years of experience and
genuine affection had gone into this work of his.

'It's all very well,' Charles would say on the way home,
staggering under the weight of his present, 'but when I go
through customs at Nice airport, they all think it's stuffed
with a load of ruddy time-bombs.'

And then one day, not long after the fiftieth anniversary celebrations, we were all standing outside the baker's house once more. This time in deep silence, we were waiting for his coffin to be lifted into the village hearse.

Two days before, early one morning, he had been found dead in the bakehouse, in front of the oven.

CHAPTER 19

Land Ablaze

SUMMER crept into July and the heat increased as the days went by. Down it came in the morning, dropping out of the furnace of the sky, and spreading over the desiccated land. By midday it was kicking back from the ground as well. Caught between the two sources, from above and below, we ached and panted as we toiled.

The high grass had turned to hay, the thorns and brambles were like barbed wire, but in spite of it all it was still growing like some ghastly science-fiction weed, feeding on cosmic rays alone. As there had been no rain since February, it was imperative to keep the ground clear on account of the bushfires raging all round. The Baou behind was blazing. The flames, creeping down the mountain like lava, were getting close to the cultivated land, driven towards us by the north wind. Great black clouds of smoke churning overhead dropped smuts and white ash all round. Three Canadairs, coming in from the sea, droned overhead on their way to the Baou. From where we stood, the aircraft seemed to skim the top of the flames as clouds of frothing water came spewing out of their bellies. By evening, that particular fire was out. Reeking black smoke oozed out of the mountainside and the smell of burning filled the air.

Next day the wind, which had dropped during the night, was roaring once more, blowing in all directions, with rival blasts of mistral and tramontane meeting head on. The seven o'clock news announced that Grasse was surrounded, and the local mental hospital had been evacuated, as the flames were running up the walls of the building. The blaze had already swept through Auribeau, Peymenade and all the surrounding villages.

It was then that people began ringing up to report on their own operations in the firing line of their advancing furnace. There was no other way but to fight your own battle, as there were far too few *pompiers* around to cope with such an emergency. Garrett called from Le Tignet to say that his house was surrounded by flames. I told him to load the family into his Land Rover, charge through the fire barrier and drive over with all the sleeping bags he could find. He agreed, if it became unavoidable, but they wanted to fight it out if they could. And all through the night, the intrepid family hosed down the burning trees and grass, and kept the house soaked and dripping. By dawn the wind had lost some of its fury, and the flames finally stopped a hundred metres away.

Then came Mike, ringing up from his bastide near Grasse. His wall of flame, advancing steadily, was still a mile off, but the whole commotion had given him palpitations, and he was going to bed, fire or no fire. Someone else in Monte Carlo said that 'Tête de Chien' behind the town was blazing. The Principality, ringed by fire, was cut off from the rest of the world. My French cousins, Chantal and Robert, arriving from Paris for a holiday in Cap d'Ail, appeared just in time to stop the fire invading their garden. All through the night they worked with buckets and hoses to keep disaster at bay. Some time during the night a couple of *pompiers* dropped in and said, 'You're doing fine, just keep going.'

As the great blaze around Grasse and Cannes began to wane, the Canadairs set off towards the Alps. A moronic peasant had lit a bonfire in his garden near Eze. Within seconds, flying sparks had set the vegetation alight and the surroundings were aflame, out of control. The fire literally flew up and down the hills all round, gobbling up the paper-dry scrub as it went. A bush fire usually travels upwards, climbing towards the top. But in this case it reversed its habits and skipped across the road, then down the hill, towards the sea. The bridges over the railway line at Eze-sur-Mer were calcinated, all electrical wiring wrecked. As a result, the road was closed for a year.

Those who saw it burning, said the village of Eze looked like a huge flaming torch. The trees and bushes growing out of the cracks in the ramparts sizzled away merrily to the top of the walls, rushed into the narrow streets, and within minutes the entire village was ablaze. There were casualties, mostly among the elderly, who could not get out of the house in time, and 2000 were made homeless. The damage was so appalling that the local mayor sent out an appeal for those who had lost everything. Government assistance was promised, but by the time this materialized the victims would have expired from want, had it not been for voluntary help.

The cloud of smoke over the coastal area grew daily. Everything was covered with ash. The stink of burning in the air was nauseating. In the end, when the wind finally dropped and the fires died down, the Prime Minister made a solemn pronouncement. Provence was to blame, he said, for her antiquated fire-fighting methods. Walkie-talkies dated from the last war. Hoses were too short. Fire-fighting aircraft were so dilapidated that they were dropping out of the sky. All of which we knew only too well, and which could have been avoided with help from the government, which was never produced.

Brittany, the only province to make an effort, sent a few *pompiers* to help their southern colleagues. But they were kept two days on the train, for a journey which took a few hours. Half-dead on arrival they were in no state to help anyone.

There are 10,000 hectares of forest and maquis burnt to cinders every year in Provence. A wood takes several generations at the very least to grow again. Wildlife, in some places, never recovers. But it would be far worse without the unstinting dedication of the fire services.

The water bombers criss-cross the sky incessantly all through the hottest months. During a crisis of this kind, the pilots hardly get any sleep, as the machines fly non-stop round the clock. There is very little time for engine maintenance or repair. As one of the most dangerous peacetime jobs, whatever the state of the weather, the little aircraft are expected to skim the surface of the sea, fill their water tanks and go straight back into the heart of the furnace. As all who live down here know only too well, gale-force winds always blow at the height of the bushfire season. And yet, in spite of almost impossible conditions, these heroic men are expected to carry on their missions as a matter of course. When a crash occurs, and the entire crew is lost, a slight frisson goes through the media, but that is as far as it goes. The service is expected to carry on as if nothing had happened.

At the height of the emergency I decided to go out on one of those operations myself to see how it worked. And so I rang up the Chief of Civil Security at Nice airport.

'No,' said the Inspecteur at the end of the line. 'We can't give you a ride in one of our machines. The last colonel in charge of the squadron got the sack for doing just that.'

'But I don't want a joy-ride,' I wailed. 'I want to write a feature about the wonderful job you do, for an English magazine . . .'

'I'm sorry, it's out of the question, but come and see me tomorrow, and I will show you round and tell you all about it.'

So next day I drove down to the airport, where an inspector had to pick me up at Frontier Police Control, as they would not let me drive off across the airstrip on my own.

As we raced through the quivering waves of heat vibrating all over the tarmac, a helicopter was just taking off on operation. All Canadairs were back over Grasse and Cannes, dealing with the tail end of the holocaust.

In the gloom of a vast shed, a battered old helicopter was being serviced by a couple of mechanics.

'These machines are quite old now,' said the Inspector. 'They constantly need updating.'

'Why not buy new ones?' I asked.

'We don't get the funds. It comes to 6600 francs an hour just to stay up in the air, not counting wages, insurance or anything else.'

I peered into the cabin of the old chopper. An ammunition box left over from the last war and filled with a first-aid kit had been screwed into the roof. Ropes and canvas bags lay on top of an ambulance stretcher on the floor. A small electric motor for winding the lifeline was a recent addition.

'A great improvement on the old system of throwing a rope through the door,' said the Inspector.

Not long ago, casualties were strapped to the landing skids beneath the cabin. As they couldn't be reached by the doctor during the flight, they were often found dead on arrival. Bitter cold, heart attacks, lack of oxygen finished them off on the way to hospital. Another casualty, rescued from his own suicide, unravelled himself and leaped into space to finish off the interrupted job.

Hanging on hooks screwed into the cabin's underbelly were huge canvas bags for dropping water in difficult spots. It could all have been designed by Heath Robinson and knocked together fifty years ago.

The heroic pilots of these helicopters are all trained by the Army or the Navy. Added to the usual nerves of steel essential for this kind of job is a spirit of inventiveness, on-the-spot decision-making, adaptability, willingness to try anything in impossible situations and incredible pluck and daring. These machines are called to all kinds of emergencies, such as the snowed-up villages cut off from the world that I keep coming across in impossible corners of the Alps. Stranded climbers and skiers are whisked away on the lifeline. Shipwrecks, floods, and, of course, the present emergency are frequent customers as well. Working hand in hand, or wing to wing with them, are the water bombers based at Marignane.

'The fire-fighting squadron came together in 1963 with Catalinas and Canadairs presented by the Canadian government. 'This force looked more like a flock of pterodactyls than an aircraft squadron when they arrived,' said the Inspector and added, 'All dating from the last war. Two of them have crashed already this month. Both crews lost as usual.'

'I know. How can such a thing happen?' I asked, harrowed by the tale of woe.

'Only too easily, I'm afraid. Releasing the water takes split-second timing. Dropping to a height of forty metres, the craft rushes past at 240 kilometres an hour, often rocking like a fallen feather, or sucked down by the vacuum of the furnace. It is touch and go. Only human judgement can be counted on, as instruments go haywire at the bucking of the plane, straining against the down-pull of airholes.'

Strange accidents occur with these water bombers. One of the pyromaniacs who crop up every summer in these parts was busy setting a mountainside on fire as a Canadair happened to be cruising overhead. Before the man could get away, down came the five and a half ton load of water over him, washing both his ears clean off his head. On another occasion, the headless corpse of a scuba diver in wetsuit and flippers was found in the bushes, picked up in the sea by the water bomber and dropped into the heart of the fire. But the real mystery is how a grown man could have been sucked into the container through the 20 by 28 centimetres slit in the tank.

According to the Inspector, 90 per cent of the fires are started deliberately. Fire services often attract arsonists into their ranks. It seems that far more people than you would ever believe are morbidly fascinated by fire. From the initial crackling, to the possible roasting of some poor wretch unable to escape, these perverts enjoy the whole range of the emotions they crave.

A young visiting fireman, here on location as extra help, was caught in the act, after setting off ten new fires which he duly reported once they were going nicely. These maniacs are incredibly ingenious in their methods. Some set up delayed-action bombs with a lighted cigarette in the middle of a toilet roll (in Corsica they use a dry cowpat). Others hang a match-box in the woods, where it will rub against tree trunks in the wind, until the 'bomb' explodes into flames.

Plain thoughtlessness can also cause terrible damage, such as shepherds firing dead grass to help the growth of new shoots for their flocks. Revenge can also be a motive among these emotional Southerners, who hate as passionately as they love. Even children do their bit, like the couple of six-year-olds who set grass alight just to see fire engines at work. Picnickers by the roadside are another menace. Cigarette ends carelessly tossed into the grass are fatal. But one myth the Inspector exploded for me was broken glass. It does *not* act as a magnifier for the sun to ignite the surrounding bush.

The Département des Eaux et Forêts explain that vegetation burns more exuberantly nowadays, because the original pri-meval trees and the slow-burning oaks have been largely replaced by Maritime and Aleppo pines. These, planted for their resin at the beginning of the century, have transformed the South of France into one huge turpentine reservoir waiting to be set alight. However, as is usual when things get out of hand through the fault of man, Nature finds a way to restore the balance. Since the early sixties a tiny bug, unknown until then, has taken over the woodlands and is busy nibbling away at the dangerous trees. So far 240,000 hectares of pines have been ravaged.

Matsococcus is the name of the little champion, without whose help our local fires would have been even more devastating.

The sun had long since set behind the reeking black cloud of smoke over Cannes in the west. As the Inspector drove me back to Frontier Control, I said: 'One last question. Do you think it is worth going to Marignane and asking for a tour in one of their Canadairs?'

'Not a hope in Heaven or Hell. The Préfet would never allow it. I am afraid that's a non-starter.' And we left it at that.

A few days later, as I was chatting with Prince Rainier's Chancellor about this first-class fire service, I told him how disappointed I was about not being allowed to go on one of their operations.

'You want to go up in a Canadair?' he asked.

'More than anything else in the world at the moment,' I said fervently. 'But I'm afraid it's impossible. The Préfet would never allow it.'

'What makes you think that? Just leave it to me. I'll fix it for you.'

'Could you *really* do it?'

'Of course it can be done.'

And one morning soon after, the Chancellor's voice came over the phone from the Palace. 'I've got your permission for you,' he said. 'You will have to get in touch with Sécurité Civile at Marignane airport. They are expecting your call.'

I rang up at once, and the date was fixed. The captain I spoke to even said he looked forward to seeing me.

CHAPTER 20

Firemen in the Sky

WHEN I finally arrived at Marignane airport near Marseilles, the policeman on duty at Securité Civile looked at me suspiciously. 'I have an appointment with the Colonel. He said he would pick me up here.' And I gave him my name.

'I'll have to see your papers.' When I handed them over he added, 'I will keep your driving licence until you leave the premises.' And only then would he ring up the control office.

Within minutes the Colonel was there to pick me up. Driving straight to the airfield, he gave me a conducted tour of the squadron. Neatly lined up on the runway were the canary-coloured Canadairs and the bright red and white Trackers in all their gleaming glory. A Fokker 27, with a huge water tank screwed into its belly like a massive kangaroo pouch, looked unfamiliar.

'It carries 3250 litres, which drop over the fire in one and a half seconds,' the Colonel told me. Having seen this many times, I knew that a fire will either snuff out instantly, or else, stimulated by the sudden oxygen intake, explode into a sky-high conflagration of bright orange flames. When that happens, the aircraft, caught up in the explosion, dives straight into the heart of the fire.

'Fokkers and Trackers have to be hose-filled on land, unlike Canadairs, which always fill up at sea,' he said, and he showed me the minute filling holes of the tanks on either side of the fuselage.

'How can those huge tanks fill up through such tiny holes in the few seconds it takes?' I asked.

'All to do with the speed of the craft hurtling over the surface of the water. You will see for yourself in a moment.'

We climbed the iron stairs up to his office. 'As you see, we're rather short of space. Only just moved in.' It all seemed fine to me. A perfectly workmanlike operational control room.

'To put you in the picture, I am in charge of operations, with the help of four other officers.' It appears that the airbase is responsible for all teaching, training and maintenance of the crews and their craft. 'But operational briefing, who is to go to which fire zone and so on, is done by CIRRCOST, at Valabre,' said the Colonel.

'What on earth is that?'

'It stands for Centre Inter-Régional de Renseignements et de Commandements Opérationnels de la Sécurité Civile.' (There are so many words in the French language, I suppose they have to be fitted in somewhere.)

'Our crews are on call throughout the summer, with twenty-seven to twenty-eight craft ready to take off any minute of the day or night. A very exhausting job. Stress is just as bad while waiting around as on operations. The station doctor regularly takes the crews' blood pressure. That's how we know. But this is not to undervalue the heroism of the crews on operation,' the Colonel pointed out. 'You will see for yourself just how strenuous, when you go through the same routine that they do on operational flights.'

At the sound of this I felt an apprehensive twitch squirming in my middle regions. He went on relentlessly, 'You can imagine what it's like in the heart of the blaze, with the flames, and the smoke and the wind. People run, scream and shout contradictory information and instructions. There is panic everywhere. Dozens of voices come over the radio, come this way, my house is on fire, there are people trapped in the woods, and so on.'

'Yes, I can imagine,' I said, as the vivid, horrific scenes reeled off through my mind.

'Is there an age limit for the crews?'

'None at all, as long as the men are in perfect physical condition. But to return to water bombers. This is the only airbase in France, going for twenty-five years. And we desperately need helicopters. But these are more expensive to maintain and to crew than planes. You can get a straight flying licence for fifteen thousand francs, but for a chopper it is four or five times more.'

'Why is that?'

'Because it's so much more tricky to handle than an ordinary aircraft. And no fire can be put out completely by a plane alone. It can take a couple of hours hovering around, watching out for that tiny flame which escaped the big drench and will start a new blaze if not stamped out.'

These men are true heroes. Their gruelling, dangerous work only gets into the limelight when one of their craft crashes into a fire, killing the crew.

'What sort of staff have you got here?' I asked.

'Altogether 210 on the base, which includes 52 pilots and 32 navigators and mechanics. There are only 100 water bombers in the world. We have one-third of them in France and the rest are in the United States, Canada and Australia. The very small number in Italy, Spain, Portugal, Greece and Turkey are all under Army control.'

The Colonel stood up. 'And now, I will hand you over to your pilot.'

He introduced me to a dashing young man with fair hair and green eyes. Clad from head to foot in a bright orange flying suit, he had a map in his hand. 'I thought you would like to see our round for today,' he said. 'We will go to St Raphaël and fill up in the bay. Then to Lérins island, so you can see the difference between still water and the high seas. We will push on to Cannes and fill up again there, then on to St Cassien and do a few somersaults over the lake. After that I will fly you back to Nice airport and drop you off there.'

'That will be wonderful,' I said, greatly relieved at not having to go all the way back to Marseilles and scramble for the last train home.

'What on earth do you want to do this crazy thing for?' he asked, as if it was the most outlandish request in the world.

I tried to explain how fascinated I was by their unconventional, adventurous way of life and the unique, flamboyant character of their work. 'Of course, I would much rather go on a real fire-fighting operation, but I know that's not possible.'

'Don't worry, we'll go through everything we ever have to do under operational conditions.'

'You mean *all* the tricks of the trade?'

'Absolutely all. But you'd better have a few of these, just in case.' And he handed me a bundle of air-sickness bags.

'Thanks,' I said. 'The Colonel told me that even pilots used them sometimes.'

'It has been known to happen.'

'Tell me about conditions, hours of work and so on. Things are pretty bad at the moment, aren't they?'

'Well, at the height of the summer, that's to be expected. It goes on day after day, without a break. And that does build up a bit.'

'How long do you have to train before you can go out on missions?'

'We are all ex-Army pilots of course. When we get here, we are in training for a year before qualifying as fully fledged water-bomber pilots. And here is your Mae West. No need to put it on. Plenty of time if we crash in the sea. And I think they want you to sign an insurance in case we drown you. Let's go and get it over, then we'll be off.'

I signed, and was interested to see that my life was insured for 300,000 francs. This done, we were joined by the navigator and went back to the landing strip. By then the sky had completely clouded over, and a few drops of rain splashed around noisily. We climbed into the cockpit.

'This is the *point fixe*,' said the captain, rapidly twiddling all the switches. The navigator crawled to the back to see if the tail was in order. Back in the cockpit, he went down on his knees to peer through a little hole in the floor. This seemed to be OK too.

'Just stand behind my seat while we take off,' said the Captain. 'And our friend will find you something to sit on.' So I clung to the back of his seat for dear life as we shot off straight up into the sky.

'OK now,' said the navigator. 'I'll find your stool.' This he squeezed between their two seats and handed me a pair of earphones. Once tightly crammed in my place, I had a stunning view through the plastic cubicle of the cabin.

'Here is our escort coming up on the right. Can you see him?' asked the Captain.

'Oh yes, he's catching up. He's going faster than we are.'

'Oh no he's not!' he flicked a switch, and our escorting Canadair dropped out of sight.

Through the earphones I could hear the Captain's voice, 'St Maximin over there. And here is Brignolles coming up. We'll go straight on to St Raphaël and fill up in the bay. Are you OK?'

'Absolutely fine.'

We cruised on for a while, with the two men's voices checking the various controls.

'Are you still OK?' the Captain asked again, looking over his shoulder. What on earth did he expect?

'Enjoying every minute, thank you.'

'Well, hold tight, we're going to scoop up water in the bay,'

We dropped like a stone through the sky, and the plane turned over. Instead of clouds, we now had the sea overhead.

'Still all right?'

'Never been better. Beautiful colour, isn't it?'

'We never push our machines or our passengers beyond what they can take,' he said. I couldn't help wondering what more he *could* do with his machine. This was a very different cup of tea from flying Air France or British Airways.

Half a second later came an almighty crash. The whole structure shuddered, creaked and rattled. My head felt as if it had been whipped off its stalk. I remembered the Colonel saying, 'Those little aircraft are rather fragile, you know.' Fragile indeed! Nothing short of a tank could have stood up to that head-on collision with the water.

We leaped upward, and immediately dropped down again, hitting the sea at 240 kilometres an hour. We were drowned in spray. The windscreen wipers whirred like mosquito wings. 'We are just filling up now – one thousand, two thousand, three thousand litres,' he rattled off as the needles shot up on the tank's clockface.

'There's the other Canadair. Can you see him on the left, down on the water?'

Our escort, graceful as a dragon-fly was touching down within an enormous plume of spray rising all round. Seconds later we watched him shooting straight up into the air as he dropped his load. We followed, circled at right angles to the water and straightened out. 'Still OK? Right, now I am un-loading.' As the water fell out of our undercarriage we swooped up vertically into the sky like a lift gone mad. This time I left my innards behind.

As we were on a routine exercise, we repeated the entire performance twice more. But the swell was getting worse, and the Captain announced that we had taken enough knocks. 'We'll go up to the mountains and do a bit of low flying. Then we'll go to the islands and fill up there.'

Heading for the hills we curled over a cliff, skimming the treetops, and he said, 'You see that house over there, we'll just go and take a look at it.' And we dived straight at the roof, missing the chimneystack by inches.

'How high are we?' I asked.

'Twenty or thirty metres.'

'Speed?'

'Two hundred and forty kilometres. And now, off to the islands.' We cut across country.

'Is that Mougin over there?' asked the Captain, pointing at a village on top of a sharp peak to the right.

The navigator peered through his window. 'It looks like it . . . Yes, yes, it is. Veer a bit to the left.'

'You navigate by sight?' I asked.

'Oh yes, we know the whole area inside out.'

'Have you read the books of St Exupéry?' I asked. At which they both smiled broadly. We were silent for a few minutes, all of us thinking about the legendary pioneer, and I felt quite nostalgic for the early days of aviation. But these space-age water-bomber pilots, in their own way, do have the best of both worlds. All the adventurous freedom and excitement of early flying days, and at the same time the most up-to-date instruments and technique if they want it. On an exercise like this, the pilot was given no instructions of any kind. He worked out his own course and decided on the length of time he would stay in the air. As we approached each town, he simply tuned into the control tower and told them what he was planning to do. And that was that.

We were now once more over the water in the Bay of Cannes. 'We will just go down and see what it looks like,' said the Captain. And over we rolled full circle. But this time it was no longer the glorious blue of St Tropez. The huge rollers billowing over our heads were an angry khaki-coloured swell that heaved and splashed about in all directions. Rushing headlong, we skimmed it once more. The shock was enough to shatter a dozen tanks. But our sturdy little machine came through in once piece. 'It's too rough,' said the Captain. 'We didn't even get a thousand litres. We will go over to the islands.'

Just missing the monastery tower, we banked over St Honorat and belly-flopped on water as smooth as a dinner table. The plane hardly shuddered. Climbing again at once, we dropped our load and shot up skyward with our usual release-bounce.

'And now,' said the Captain, 'I suppose we will have to head for Nice. I wanted to take you into the mountains, but with all these heavy clouds about, we wouldn't see a thing.'

Landing a few minutes later at Nice airport, we taxied into the Civil Security compound. Although the place looked totally deserted, I knew that the Inspector would be up in his lair. We climbed the iron staircase to the control office and, sure enough, there he was, surrounded by a bevy of flying men in their bright orange overalls.

'May I introduce Madame de St Albans?' said the Captain.

'Oh, but we are old friends!' exclaimed the Inspector, goggling at me.

'In that case, will you escort her back to the security checkpoint? And she can tell you all about our afternoon.'

The Inspector drove me back to the main airport and dropped me off at the coach stop, just as the Monte Carlo bus drew up. It was all going like clockwork.

And so ended the most exciting birthday I have ever had in my life.

CHAPTER 21

Goodbye to All That,
Once Again

By the end of the summer all fires were out, but the entire region was calcinated, with a few black tree stumps sticking up here and there and not a leaf in sight. The cold weather settled in unusually early, and on a bright November morning, as I set off to market, there was hoarfrost on the grass and the lower branches of the mimosa trees. It was Friday, and the streets were already jammed with noisy, bustling crowds when I got there.

As ants rush to jam, I am irresistibly drawn to fairs and markets wherever I go. The bright colours of the stalls, the smell of herbs and spices, fish and fruit, the merchants bawling out the virtues of their wares, the deafening clamour and general uproar, always bring back the excitement of early youth and the bazaars of the East.

The fish stalls I navigated around that morning heaved and creaked with live crabs and lobsters crawling over one another and falling overboard, cracking their skulls on the pavement and losing one or two claws in the process. One hefty fellow was heading off towards the sea ten miles away, with nobody paying the slightest attention. A huge wild boar, shot between the eyes, lay sprawling over an orange box. Next to him was a pile of Nigerian drums made of elephant hide and an intriguing bunch of assegais. Cartridge belts, hunting knives and boots hung from the branches of a pepper tree. At a clothes stall a boy of about fifteen was choosing a pair of jeans with his mother. Closely watched by her and the merchant, he dropped his trousers and struggled into a pair of jeans at least two sizes too small. Flattening himself with his left hand, he battled with the zip, but, pull as he might, he couldn't get it over the hump.

'He's got everything he needs there,' remarked the mother proudly, patting the obstruction. 'Only fifteen, would you believe it, and look at him already!'

'Ah well, you can't have it everywhere,' said the merchant. 'When there's not too much upstairs, you might as well have it there.'

The air was nippy, and those who were undressing to try something on stepped into patches of sunshine. Under a plane tree a station wagon with the owner's skis clipped to the roofrack was festooned with pullovers, slacks, skirts and dresses. The man himself kept warm inside at the wheel, the window closed. A bottle of wine stood on the dashboard, and with a thoughtful look he carved off slices of *saucisson*, which he popped into his mouth on the end of his knife. Whenever a customer banged on his window, he wound it down and conducted the sale from his seat.

At a busy cheese stall a housewife, wrapped up to the eyeballs, grumbled about the weather. 'I think it's even colder than last year. My feet have turned to ice.'

'Well,' said the mature dairymaid behind her cheese, 'you've got a fine gentleman just behind you in the queue. He should be able to keep you warm.'

'Oh, he would have a job to do it – wouldn't be up to it, just look at him,' she said, turning to glare at the 'fine gentleman'.

'I'm a strong man, I'll have you know,' said he, bristling. 'Besides, I'm Italian, not one of your puny Frenchmen.'

'I'd gobble you up in two bites. There'd be nothing left of you,' said the woman scornfully. And with that she rattled her basket on wheels, and rammed it into his legs to get him out of the way.

The man then turned to me. As I was having trouble keeping a straight face, I quickly looked away. So instead he addressed the cheerful old peasant across her cheeses. 'Well, let's have a smile from you, at least.'

'That would cost you dear, my little man.'

'At your age? Come on, you're just an old crone. An old smile costs nothing.'

'Ha! That's where you're wrong! It's like wine. The older the better. Real vintage, so there. And what can I give you today?'

Further along, at a fruit stall, the merchant was saying, 'And how is the poor man today?'

'He must be in a terrible state,' answered a customer with relish. 'He is having an awful job to get her buried. It's not as if she was a Christian. You see, she was Protestant!'

These markets and fairs started in the earliest days of the history of mankind. In fact, I am always amazed that so many have survived to this day, in spite of the worldwide epidemic of supermarkets. But, of course, the great international trading centres of the Middle Ages, the huge spring and autumn fairs on which European commerce depended entirely, have long ago disappeared.

At the great market of Beaucaire, where over 100,000 merchants and buyers turned up every year, the first barge sailing up the river to arrive at the appointed time received a prize from the town of a sheep and a barrel of wine. It is difficult nowadays to imagine the splendour of these enormous gatherings, which took place all over Provence, as late as the eighteenth century. You could literally find anything at these fairs, from diamonds, cloth of gold, horseflesh, right down to tutors and teachers for your children. The long winter evenings in the high valleys of the Alps provide plenty of time for reading and studying. In those days, apart from carving wild animals out of pinewood, there was little else to do. Reading, therefore, was a pastime, for those who knew how. As a result, teachers were much in demand in the mountain districts. Knowing where they would find takers, these Alpine academics would flock to the fairs to offer their services – in code, with feathers. Sticking out of the hatband, one feather meant, 'can read and write', two announced, 'know Latin', and three stood for 'can do mathematics'. All you had to do was to know the code, and the situation was clear to all concerned.

Meanwhile, on the stroke of twelve, our own market in Vence was packing up. The stalls were vanishing at incredible speed, and I knew that within half an hour there would be no sign left of the morning's intense activity.

It was time for me to make tracks for home.

As usual, the sun was intensely hot. But in the shade it was very cold. So, by moving the table away from the shade of the cypress trees, we were still able to eat out of doors. Alan and Nad, home for the weekend, were making themselves useful with cushions and chairs, while Pierre officiated at the barbecue as usual. Hot and tired after my long walk from the village, I was glad of the glass of wine that Charles handed me.

By three o'clock everybody was back at work. I sat at the garden table, banging away at my typewriter. A blackbird, perched on a telephone wire, repeated the sound of every key I hit. When I stopped to think, he peered down to see what was happening. As soon as I started again, off he went once more, ratatat tat. It was like two machines going on at the same time.

Anne sat in the grass, darning cigarette holes in Alan's jersey with one of Nad's long blond hairs. 'Can I have another one?' she said from time to time. And Nad, who was boning up on women in French literature for her thesis, pulled a long shiny hair out of her head without looking up and handed it over. Her heavy mane, hanging out to dry over the back of her chair, looked like the Golden Fleece, shooting sparks at the setting sun.

The evening passed off with no more worries than having to cope with the usual smoke of the dining-room fire. There was no sign, no premonition of the tragedy that was about to strike.

At around 2 a.m., Anne banged on our bedroom door shouting, 'Pierre is dead. Get up, hurry up, I tell you he is *dead*!'

We leaped out of bed and into our clothes. Wrenching the door open, I pulled Anne in and sat her on my bed. 'Look after her,' I said to Charles, 'I'm going to get a doctor.'

Rushing to the telephone, I dialled Service de Secours, the Vence emergency number. No reply. I tried again and again. There was no one there. The equivalent number in Nice, which I dialled next, said they could not help.

'This is a matter of life and death,' I pleaded.

'That's no reason at all,' said the voice. 'Our doctor doesn't go out of Nice.'

'What shall I do, for goodness' sake? This is desperately urgent.'

'Try the Vence number again, there should be someone there.' So I had another go. Still no reply. Once more I rang up Nice. 'Try the police,' snapped the voice, and rang off. I tried the police and hung on for ages. No reply. There was only one thing to do. I jumped into the Mini and raced down to the village. In the window of the police station, a notice was propped up on a chair saying, 'In case of emergency ring up Cagnes police station.'

I tore across the car park to the public callbox. There, the handpiece had been wrenched right off the machine.

There were still the chemists. One of them ought to be on night duty. But all three were barred and locked. No light anywhere. Stunned and dazed, I stood helplessly in the middle of the road, wondering what to do next.

At that moment, Charles and Anne, who had followed in her Daf, emerged from the Café de la Victoire on the corner. A waiter was piling chairs on the terrace tables. 'Ring up the *pompiers*,' he said, 'yes, use our phone. Didn't anybody tell you? It's always the *pompiers* who deal with this kind of emergency.'

Within seconds, the local fire engine was in the square, asking for directions. The captain in charge got into the Mini beside me, and we led the way. The great roaring engine followed, with the Daf in the tail. Up the hill we toiled, rattling and stalling on the loose stones of the track. At the house, the firemen brought in a couple of oxygen tubes and a stretcher from their engine. The doctor rushed inside and we all followed.

Half an hour later they were downstairs again. The doctor spoke to Anne, and one of the firemen said to me, 'We could see when we arrived that it was too late, but we tried everything all the same.' Numb with shock, we stood around, speechless. 'Give her an injection,' I said to the doctor in the end. 'Please do that at least.'

Along with their airborne colleagues, the *pompiers* of France are the most dedicated, energetic and effective public service in the land. Always turning up at once, never grumbling, whatever the problem, from a regular fire to a sudden death or a hornets' nest. They are kindly, sympathetic and compassionate. As I turned round, a big burly fellow with a walrus moustache had his arms around Anne, as she sobbed on his shoulder.

The next day we launched a new house-painting scheme. And for a week we splashed walls and ceilings furiously, trying not to think. Anne's fortitude was awe-inspiring. The worst time of the day was stopping for meals. Then we really had to face up to it.

A few days later, just before I woke up, Pierre appeared to me in a dream. Looking twenty years younger, with a healthy tan and his face filled out, he breezed into the bedroom in his old raincoat. 'Don't worry so much about me,' he said. 'It's very nice where I am. Very much like here, but everybody is lighter, and there is no mischief or backbiting. None of the malice you have down here. I am often around with you, but you can't see me.'

After that, I grieved much less.

A couple of weeks later Anne, still in a state of shock, went to the town hall to offer her body after death for medical research. She came back fuming with indignation.

'I had to fill in half a dozen forms, with all the usual great-grandmothers' maiden names and so on. Then, just as I was leaving, the clerk said to me, "Just a minute, madame, now you must give me eight hundred francs."'

Amazed, Anne asked what it was for. 'I am giving you my body. You don't expect me to pay for it!'

'We certainly do,' said the woman. 'You have to pay to have your body collected. We have to send a *camionnette* to pick up the corpse. Who is going to pay for that if you don't?'

I was relieved to see Anne come back to life, even if it was only to hiss and fume with indignation. She spluttered on, 'I went in to see the chief welfare officer on the way out. Thinking she would be horrified, I told her the whole story. And all she said was, "Well, I suppose eight hundred francs is rather high, but what with inflation and so on you have to expect it."'

Too distressed and wretched to settle down to normal life again, we decided to make a complete break and sell the house. We simply did not have the heart to carry on without Pierre.

In all the years since my father had built Mas Mistral, there have been a great many changes. Sir Frederick Treves, writing about the Riviera in the twenties, said the place was almost deserted. Whereas now, in the eighties, it had become a very prosperous market town, spreading out in all directions, with tower blocks going up wherever a slice of land still stood empty. The old peasant families, many of them going back to the Middle Ages, now rich from selling vineyards and carnation fields for development, owned two or three cars each and sometimes more.

Deciding to take the plunge, we put the house up for sale.

As it happened, the agent knew of a developer who was looking for a property of this kind. But in order to make it worth his while, we would have to throw in another house which we owned in the town and which was usually let.

In spite of some misgivings, we signed the contract, only to have our buyer shoot himself a few days later. Hounded and cornered by his creditors, the poor man could see no other way out of his dilemma.

Shaken by the outcome of our first attempt, we put the house in the hands of another agent, and this time the deal went through without a hitch. Moreover, we had three months' grace in which to sort out, sell or otherwise dispose of the contents of the house. This meant sixty years of accumulated possessions to be brought down from the attic, hauled up from the cellar and gathered in from the various sheds and barns behind the house. The prospect was daunting.

Finally, on a balmy winter morning, Anne and I got down to it. Altogether it took three weeks to complete the operation. When everything was finally laid out in the downstairs flat, the place looked like one enormous junk shop. Day after day, we cruised back and forth among the outlandish hoard, viewing it all with a baleful eye.

'The first thing to do is to sort out the pure junk from all the bronze and silver antiques,' I said.

And we began to shift all my father's Chinese and Japanese treasures into one corner. Anne's African lot, Benin bronzes, goddesses, carved buffalo horns, ivory knick-knacks and hippo drums, went into a room of their own. The heavier Provençal furniture was shunted into the hall for storing in our old cellars at La Turbie. After that, we drove down to the village, to call on the antique shops. The owner of the Furniture Cave in the main square agreed to come and have a look at our collection.

'What prices do you want?' she asked.

'We have no idea. We thought you might like to make an offer.'

'You are saying you want a free estimate. Not on your life. Go and do your own pricing, then let me know when you've finished.'

So back we went to cope with the job. It took us a week to get through it all.

'And now I suppose we'd better get down to those files,' said Anne, dragging a great pile of them towards her. We plunged into the forbidding mountain of paper. Old X-rays, hospital and funeral bills went straight into a box for burning. And so did building permits, acrimonious letters from neighbours and old school reports. There were press cuttings of my father's short stories published in various magazines and newspapers around the world. These we set aside, along with my mother's diaries, containing the quaint and inane sayings of our extreme youth. Then came a menu card of the first Christmas dinner they had eaten in the house. My father had painted a black cobra with outspread wings on the card (a cobra for Christmas, typical of Papa's black humour). The menu, dated 1921, listed the delicacies they had eaten that evening –*hors d'oeuvres, dinde truffée, asperges glacées, foie gras,* plum pudding, *macedoine de fruits au champagne,* liqueurs. Among the signatures on the back are those of Henri Fauconnier and his wife Madeleine.

In the end, exhausted and thoroughly depressed, we grabbed a bottle of wine and sat down with it on the front step in the setting sun.

'What's happened to our old rocking horse?' I suddenly asked. 'It should have been in the attic.'

'I don't remember it. But Abbé Pierre was here a few years ago. He took a whole lorry load of stuff away with him at the time.' The thought that anyone had already had a go at the attic seemed preposterous.

It was getting cold. The sun had left the step where Anne and I sat, middle-aged and grizzled, where we had so often perched half a century earlier, ostensibly learning our lessons but, more often than not, reading comics.

Shades of the past and long-laid ghosts came drifting round the house. Our formidable nanny, whose undertaker's contract for a grave 'in perpetuity' we had just come across, would be closing the shutters upstairs, cursing the bats trying to get in. Madame Rose, the cook, would be hobbling in from the kitchen garden with a bunch of fresh herbs for dinner. And at this hour, etched against the orange glow of the horizon, old Rubio, the Spanish manservant, could usually be seen loping along with an armful of logs, to keep the smoke of the dining-room fire choking us all throughout the evening.

Full of wine and nostalgia, Anne and I got up reluctantly and tottered into the house to cook the family dinner.

Meanwhile Charles had been busy buying a small house on the southern ramparts of the town, overlooking the coastline between Cagnes and Antibes.

The remaining furniture that had not gone into storage in our cellars at La Turbie was ferried down the hill in Arduin's van and installed in the town house by the weekend.

From then on it became easier to start a new life. The municipal road drill came over to excavate a swimming pool out of the garden rock and, tethering himself once more to his machine, Charles mowed away the waist-high grass around the house. And within a few hours we were surrounded by quite respectable lawns.

But Anne needed to spread her wings still further. After Christmas she left for Australia, where to this day she lives in her Queensland bungalow, surrounded by lawns and swimming pool, with parrots and cockatoos fluttering about among the ghost gums and flame trees of her garden.